The
R.O.C.K.Y
PROJECT

ISBN: 9798756032604

Imprint: Independently published

This book was produced in collaboration with Write Business Results Limited. For more information on their business book, blog and podcast services, please visit **www.writebusinessresults.com** or contact the team via **info@writebusinessresults.com**.

The
R.O.C.K.Y
PROJECT

FIRST EDITION

Michael Bibb

ACKNOWLEDGMENTS

This book would not have been possible without the following tribe who have helped me on this journey, they have coached me, challenged me, suffered with me and helped us arrive at what, for me, is Alchemy. Packing together, never dreamt of/ undiscovered experience and collected worldly wisdom into this little book, to have a massive impact on your life:

Jason Bibb – Little Cuz, we are brothers, thanks for all the adventures and already looking forward to the next one with you.

Bazza – thanks for believing in me from the off.

Dom West – having you in my corner and writing my foreword when you are in the middle of filming "The Crown" means a lot – thanks old friend.

Clarkey – Rockstar! Man, you have had some journey since we met on that flight to Bermuda and thanks for helping me with my journeying too.

Guildhall School of Music & Drama – for opening up a chapter in my life that was just a childhood dream but you brought me to London, to live that dream and work with amazing teachers and discover life through art.

Coventry Triathletes – for teaching me to swim at age 46 and your sky blue/blue sky thinking that made this "stocky" bloke, a multiple IRONMAN® race finisher and some.

Penny Wilkin – thanks for not laughing when I said I wanted to do three IRONMAN® races in three months!

Marathon Des Sables, Tent 52 – thank you for taking Rocky into your tent, he was much older and much slower, you made no judgement. We all did it – MDS Finishers. Thank you my boys.

The London Triathlon competitor (the Medical Race Director couldn't give me your name) – wherever you are, thank you for being that call to action, on that day in the River Thames, glad to have answered the call – for us both!

My Carpe Diem Private Clients – who wanted to work with someone who cared about more than the money, thank you for shaping me and for my coaching clients that allow me to help you, shape you. Not everyone gets to feel like Michelangelo, thanks for letting me walk with you along your journey.

The team at WBR – for giving me this jumping off place, as I may well still have been just talking about the book I am writing, instead of getting it done.

And My Family – for letting this 50-something Rocky live, to take on the IRONMAN® races and the Ultras and always to return home to love, fun and our own brand of Alchemy.

DEDICATION

To my wife and children, you are my world, so rich to have each of you in my life. I give my thanks to my Mum for her strength. My grandparents for their wisdom and telling me, time and time and again, "You can do anything you put your mind to," and thanks to God for all the blessings we receive.

CONTENTS

FOREWORD

Michael and I were at drama school together and I think it was during an exercise pretending to be a volcano that we became friends. We were a group of four men, in tights and intertwined, improvising the rumble and then explosion of Vesuvius. After the scene's climactic end, the teacher asked how it had been for us and Michael's alas unrepeatable answer was so funny that I'm still laughing now. For the rest of our three-year training, Michael was the partner I always sought out. With Michael, you were guaranteed a fruitful, often hilarious, collaboration. To work with him was and is a delight, because the humour springs from a deep well of humanity and empathy.

We were taught in those days that the essence of successful improvisation is to offer something up and then listen and build on your partner's responses. To avoid opening a scene with, "What are you doing here?" And instead offer, "What a huge hat you're wearing"; to say, "Yes and..." instead of, "No but...". It was a process of which Michael became a master. It complemented his innate warmth and seriousness and made him versatile and easily creative with all that life has thrown at him. He has embodied the director Peter Brook's exhortation to "hold on tightly... but let go lightly"; to be fully committed but deft enough to change direction. It has seen him soar as an actor, a financial adviser, a marathon runner, a writer and a life coach. To be the "laughing Buddha changing masks"; cheerfully moving on; always onwards, always upwards. It is, after all, what life's journey is all about and this inspiring book reminds us of that.

Through case studies of his own exemplars, Michael reminds us to reach for the stars and not let doubt, fear or the inevitable vicissitudes of life dissipate our dreams. He reminds us never to stop learning, never to stop seeking help, both from the heroes who inspire us and from the coaches like himself, who exist to lighten the load and carry us over the line. Above all though, he reminds us how little time we have and how absurd it is to waste that time. Because as one of my own heroes, Lord Byron, so brilliantly observed:

"When one subtracts from life infancy, sleep, eating and swilling – buttoning and unbuttoning – how much remains of downright existence? The summer of a dormouse."

Dominic West

PROLOGUE

WHY ROCKY?

Let's get one thing clear: I love Rocky. As a kid I watched Rocky (I) over and over and over. As a teen, his poster was on my wall, watching me, inspiring me. When they carry me out of this world it will be to "*Gonna Fly Now*" (Bill Conti). Even as a child the underdog drew me, fascinated me – perhaps because I was/am one. Essentially, I grew up in a single parent family, but with caring Grandparents, in mine and my Mum's corner. Mum was holding down two jobs to put food on the table, so breaking through and winning against the odds was all very real. When I saw Rocky for the first time, I knew his story; it was my story.

The Rocky we all know from the movies is not a real person. Like Sherlock Holmes, he is a work of fiction that has worked its way into our hearts and minds, so he must have lived, surely? The movie character Rocky was based on Chuck Wepner, who in 1975 was only seconds away from going the distance with Muhammad Ali. Perhaps Stallone was doffing his cap to the movie's namesake Rocky Marciano, who was born into poverty and took the hard yards to become (and still is) the undefeated Champion of the World.

This book is not about a movie, or a fight in a boxing ring, this book actually has nothing to do with boxing; it is about you, your fights and your struggles. YOU are the project, you are the work in progress and whilst you may not be hungering for your own heavyweight championship belt, you have your own challenges, your own titles that you want to achieve and to be able to say, when all is said and done, "I did that." This book is to encourage you to see yourself as the Project. Rocky is my hunting brave name, but this is about you and your alter ego/s, your hunting brave name for your journey. This is evolution or, depending on where and how you are sitting, REVOLUTION.

So much is changing in the world, many more of us are allowing ourselves to feel that there is more to be done and more we are capable of. Over these next pages I hope to demonstrate that we are, all of us, extraordinary and living in extraordinary times, and that is not just a happy thought – you will see many examples of those who not only think they can, they do.

Coming up, we'll be talking about heroes. They came from different backgrounds, they had different goals, they overcame adversity and are a torch for us all to strive towards, not just to survive but thrive. They pave the way for you to do something that will not only make you proud of yourself, but do something for the grandkids and dare I say when we are sitting on the park bench feeding the birds, it might well be these things that you never thought were in you that spontaneously make you smile and in your mind's eye say, "Yep that was me," and then shake your head, as you, for so long, thought it impossible but you did it anyway. This is about today and tomorrow, your legacy, your life – so what are you doing about it? "What have you done today to make you feel proud?" asked M People. This is not hard stuff, it is just the difference between binge watching a box set series and getting off the couch and surprising yourself – you have magic in you, let it out!

Here are some dictionary meanings and even some Latin, so you know we are getting serious:

Project (or program) as any undertaking, carried out individually or collaboratively that is carefully planned (usually) to achieve a particular aim. *project* comes from the Latin word *projectum* from the Latin verb *proicere*, "before an action".

....

rocky, *difficult* and full of problems: *the rocky road to success.*

....

iROCKY

My alter ego, my Rocky, emerged or rather showed himself proper, on The West Highland Way in 2009 when I was asked to join a team of four for The Caledonian Challenge: 54 miles in 24 hours, from Fort William to Loch Lomond. That might not sound a big deal to some but taking on The Devil's Staircase and the lonely Rannoch Moor, with little to no prep, was a baptism by fire. My hunting brave name/nickname Rocky was to stick and would lead me on to cycling across Europe, taking up the IRONMAN® race challenge, going Ultra and taking on running across the Sahara.

You have heard many before say, "If I can do it, then anyone can," and this is true. I repeat – this is true. This renaissance started back when I was 39 (yes, you read that right) and has gathered momentum since. I was never a swimmer, cyclist or runner, but what I am is an infectious positive thinker. I hope the itching starts for you as you're poring through these pages and you discover something about yourself that was hitherto denied, or just not realised. As we know, thinking alone is not enough, you need action, but if you think you can, well, you're 80 per cent there. It was many years later that the book, *The Brave Athlete:Calm the F*ck Down and rise to the Occasion* by Simon Marshall PhD and Lesley Paterson was recommended to me, where Lesley Patterson shares that she uses an alter ego for her races, and we should all choose one to get us through races! We MUST be on the right path then.

I have to confess the Rocky fanfare *"Gonna Fly Now"* has lifted me when I thought I could go no further; when I had to dig deep through unintentional dehydration, or intentional lack of training (NB I have four wonderful children and they are the best of me, so when given a choice, I choose them and the training waits for another day – this is okay for me though, as I want balance and only need to survive the races; I am not trying to win them, just beat the clock).

This life often takes you to some places you never thought you would go. Personally I have always loved acting and the theatre, it's a transportation vehicle available to all.

My dream of becoming an actor got some real traction, I went to drama school (against all odds) and did some stuff, but fast forward ten years after making that commitment to being an actor and you find me taking a temp job in a call centre, 'between' acting jobs in good old London town. Then I had an epiphany: I could be living in my London flat and getting excited about a TV job on "The Bill" and still be here, in the same flat, in ten years time, reliant on someone giving me my break. I didn't like that view, it seemed to be such a waste of time, so I decided to "do life."

The 1998 epiphany in my London flat meant that I should leave the big city and come back home, to the place of my forebears, and put down some roots. I decided that if acting was in my blood, if it was my destiny, then I would come back to it. The key lesson from this is to have a clear, massive goal, DREAM BIG! Don't just say, for example, "I want to be an actor" as all the things I dreamt actually came true. I did get to work with The Royal Shakespeare Company (RSC) and did get on the telly, I also did film, I did get to play Hamlet (I should have visualised more specifically though – "Win best actor Oscar, make 12 films that I am proud of etc"). I thought that due to where I came from, even having that dream, that impossible dream about becoming an actor for a smaller than average, and rounder than average, kid from Coventry, was dreaming big. I did get into one of the best drama schools in the world and do what I set out to do. We can always go bigger though; we can always go Ultra, as you will discover.

My adventures in acting did take me around the world, which has been great and a wonderful educator. For me, it was always about the work – a diligent student, always looking at the character's arc, journey and looking for truth! Now I find myself translating that to my clients and their truth, their journey.

INTRODUCTION

The R.O.C.K.Y Project – BUT what does that mean Michael?

This book is about journey, and for our travels together we will use some of my journey as an everyman character (iRocky), and 12 recognised heroes/champions/greats from many different fields: sports, the arts, science, politics, and the thread running through all of this will be how we can accompany you on your own journey, whether you believe you are on one, or are yet to start. Yes, there will be challenges, but like Rocky who had Mickey and then Apollo, you have your inspiration next to you, in your corner. Like Luke when he finds Obi-Wan Kenobi who gives him belief and then Yoda who teaches him what he needs to know (Star Wars) or like Neo and Morpheus (The Matrix) who wrestle so that he can, "Set you free." What I am saying is see the type of hero you are, just decide. To be clear, it isn't enough to say you are a solicitor, wealth manager, entrepreneur etc. – exams will get a few letters after your name, and are necessary to be relevant in your chosen profession, but they only get you so far; you need to know your value, your purpose.

Some navigation: at the end of each chapter we will tread side by side along The R.O.C.K.Y Road, using the life lesson/s from each of our heroes. These will look like this:

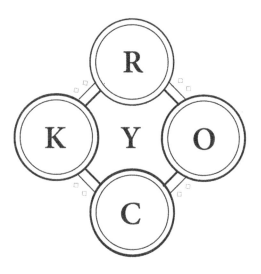

Rise – Where are you going?

Obstacle – What is in your way?

Choices – How do you get through it/over it?

Kaizen – Changing for the better/continuous improvement

You – You carry the choice to rise or reach an impasse at the obstacle/s. It is all about you – Subject of a verb or object of the verb

There is an iconic scene in Rocky that each of the films returns to and that is him at his peak, running up those famous steps in Philadelphia, getting to the top and punching the air – let us take you one step further, taking all your efforts and achievements to this point and not stopping at the top of those stairs; keep moving ahead and you will see a museum, our Museum, The MUSEum of Momentum...

Museum noun, a building in which objects of artistic, cultural, historical, or scientific interest are kept and shown to the public.

....

This represents your mind gym, your virtual boardroom with 12 new executives each bringing with them a skill, a lesson, a value to you and your ongoing challenges. It is so easy to get wrapped up in the small mindedness of some and also to get shanghaied by others' needs and wants. I'm not saying it is a bad thing, not at all, you have the evidence in this book to support helping others – it only becomes a problem when that derails you from stuff that you have to get done. That could be studying for an exam, finishing your book or doing that thing you always wanted to do, walking the Appalachian Trail, taking up Karate, water-colour painting or fly fishing in Scotland – you know what I am getting at. Both/all is the answer, but you know you could do worse than to take advice from your friendly air stewardess: put the oxygen mask on YOU first before you help others. Whatever your oxygen looks like to you, make sure that you are feeding your soul as well as enriching others.

....

ENTER THE MUSEUM OF MOMENTUM

At the end of each chapter we will visit our MUSEum of Momentum and allow our ambassadors of self discovery to speak to us; to share their gift/s and their wisdom. It's easy to enter here and go to work. It is like meditation, but with a visualisation and it's easy: pick any wall, focus on one spot, you will see a door appear (I know – like Alice in Wonderland, right?). At first you see an outline of a tiny door; go through the door and you see a horseshoe-shaped table that you can walk right into. There are 12 places at this table and each will get filled by way of a chapter/introduction in this book. Each person occupying one of those places has a quality, an essence, and it is through these visits that you will bring home the strength, inspiration or what has been alluding you all these years.

It is our mind palace, our fortress of solitude, so to speak. If Superman needs one to gather his thoughts, then the world can allow us this device to see more clearly, to listen to the voices, some of old, some contemporary and some that are just plain universal. As Superman is able to learn from the wisdom of his long departed, so too can we learn ancient wisdoms to inform our today and enrich our tomorrows.

I appreciate that this might be a challenge for some, but just try this next time you go to the gym. If you're on the treadmill and you have put in 40 minutes on the clock, but around the 10 minute mark you feel like quitting, then find your mark on the wall, see the door open and, like Alice in Wonderland, shazam you are in. Goggins, world's hardest man, is there coaching you, telling you just to get to 20 mins, you get to 20, go for 30, you get to 30 you might as well keep going now and do the full set. What happened? What has changed? You are still in the gym, you are still you, on the treadmill, the wall is just the wall. What changed is that you were able to take yourself out of yourself, away from your chimp and its rambling voice telling you about the pain and your aching joints, and that you don't have to do this running thing.

You were able to travel out of the gym and to our MUSEum of Momentum, and once there, you could regroup, refocus, recentre and listen to one of our mentors – it works and it will keep working for you until the time you decide that you are too old for this and, just like the C.S Lewis children, the wardrobe is just a wardrobe and not a portal to Narnia and adventures beyond. All it takes is a little concentration. Your imagination is one of your greatest allies, and the more you do this, the more clearly the door will appear. It is an off-white coloured door for me; yours may well be a different colour and when I am in, the ceiling is high and the 12 are there, waiting for me to visit so they can do what they do best and that is help me on my journey, as they can help you on yours. The place looks neutral, almost like a potter's studio, but the further you venture in the more the place seems to come alive. You take your challenges, your doubts and your questions there and it is this that gives this place meaning. YOU give it life. See it.

This is our thinking place – our dojo, to wrestle some of the messages of each chapter. Don't skip this though, you have to work through it – this is on you. If you are working on you and need to awaken something in you, you have to fan those flames for your phoenix to rise, I am starting the fire in you, but you have to make it burn – agreed?

Agreed.

muse (v.) reflect deeply on a subject;
Synonyms: chew over / think over / meditate / ponder / excogitate / contemplate / reflect / mull / mull over / ruminate / speculate
muse (n.) the source of an artist's inspiration;
Muse (n.) in ancient Greek mythology any of 9 daughters of Zeus and Mnemosyne; protector of an art or science

From wordnet.princeton

. . . .

Our MUSEum is a boardroom. Some Museums can feel old, ancient and stuffy; but not this one. Like Tate Modern, this is vibrant, teeming and full of life.

Imagine if this museum was dedicated to our 12 Rocky files, our ambassadors of Kaizen, our warriors of continuous improvement. The ceiling is the Sistine chapel, more importantly the back wall is our own Day of Judgement, a phoenix flies through reminding us of rebirth and that impossible, like phoenix, is just a word. We hear Churchill's voice, "Never give up, never give up, never give up!" We see Shakespeare coming to life before us, "Some are born to greatness, some achieve greatness and some have greatness thrust upon them." You see the before and after Goggins following his journey through hell and back, to tell us what is achieved even when the odds are stacked against us. There's Jane Tomlinson battling through all the endurance events with cancer and chemo raging inside her, carrying hell with her, racing always against the clock, she battles on. An aeroplane flies through the rafters with the Wright brothers waving us on, daring you to show the world what you can do. To your right, the All Blacks perform their Haka – you feel their voice, their commitment, their passion. There is the 11 year old Billie Jean King, racquet in hand and with absolute certainty, she is telling you she will be world number one. Muhammad Ali stands torch in hand, indefatigable, and Marie Curie, next to Muhammad Ali, holds a vial up. It could be that new element that she has discovered, it could be radioactive, it could be the stuff of alchemy. There's Chrissie Wellington wearing the lei of the world champ, arms aloft, radiating. Michelangelo working away, not just chipping away, but breathing life into his work.

Give yourself permission to let your imagination work the room, don't take it from me though, one of the greatest minds of our age, said this of imagination:

"Imagination is more important than knowledge. For knowledge is limited, whereas imagination embraces the entire world, stimulating progress, giving birth to evolution." (Albert Einstein)[1]

You see these can be just names to you, a selection of consonants and vowels (but aren't all names?) or they can be touchstones for you, an opportunity for you to sense-check. Jane did what? Chrissie came from nowhere? Ali wasn't always the greatest, how? BJK said what at 11 years old? And then trumped that at age 12, and she is still doing it?! Michelangelo made what with what? Marie Curie accomplished greatness as a widowed, single mum and then one of her girls goes on to win a Nobel prize too – these people leave us no hiding place.

They found their passion and pursued it against the odds. The excuses that we use for not pursuing our passion start to fade and we see them for what they are – excuses. Are you going to settle for that or will our MUSEum of Momentum peel back some of the layers you have allowed to settle over you, on your dreams, and dust them off? Never give up, never give up, never give up...

. . . .

[1] Albert Einstein, (1931), *Cosmic Religion: With Other Opinions and Aphorisms*, Covici, Friede; New York

JOIN THE MUSEUM TOUR

You will have 12 tickets to visit the MUSEum on this tour. During this time put the book down and meditate/muse there on the lesson, on the message from the exhibit we have built for you. Consider this place your Head Dojo – you get a chance to refocus here as we work with our Kaizen emissaries.

Goethe is credited with the following line, "Whatever you can do, or dream you can, begin it. Boldness has genius, power, and magic in it." Whoever said it and wherever it came from, the truth comes out. Boldness does have power and magic in it. For us to get through the fog and noise of this life and rise above the din, we must become a Battler of Confusions and that's what we will be looking for in our time together.

The MUSEum is here to help your muse by way of a regroup. This book is a travel guide, a portal. To get back to The MUSEum, take a moment or two, to, as Dr Stephen Covey puts it, "To sharpen the saw."[2] You can, of course, add your own contributors. In this book I have included 12 of my all-time Hall of Famers, looking at their stories, their struggles and their alchemy. All I ask is to make sure that those you bring to the table have earned their place and that they talk to you. Part of the magic comes from hearing the whispers in your ear, Churchill's, "Never give up, never give up, never give up!" Goggins', "Stay hard." The resounding achievements of the All Blacks and the genius of Curie.

A couple of house rules: when you pick up this book please put down any cynicism you may have (remember no one ever built a statue to a critic!) and when your brain starts saying, "Oh well it's okay for her...", "I never had those opportunities...", "I'm too old/it's too late for me," – any of these nay-sayings need to be put in a box and left there. This is a demonstration, through fact, that you CAN! Where you have some unfinished business or that, "Road not taken," (and we all have those roads) this book will help you pack up your kit bag and if there is something that needs to get done, if there is something overdue, if you want to find and walk down that road you have

[2] Stephen R Covey, (1989), *The 7 Habits of Highly Effective People*, Free Press

denied yourself for so long, then now is the time. YOU are the man or woman in the arena and the credit goes to you, and it is to the warrior in you, not the critic and not the worrier, that I and Roosevelt are calling out to:

"It is not the critic who counts; not the man who points out how the strong man stumbles, or where the doer of deeds could have done them better. The credit belongs to the man who is actually in the arena, whose face is marred by dust and sweat and blood; who strives valiantly; who errs, who comes short again and again, because there is no effort without error and shortcoming; but who does actually strive to do the deeds; who knows great enthusiasms, the great devotions; who spends himself in a worthy cause; who at the best knows in the end the triumph of high achievement, and who at the worst, if he fails, at least fails while daring greatly, so that his place shall never be with those cold and timid souls who neither know victory nor defeat." Theodore Roosevelt, 23 April 1910

. . . .

GOING THE DISTANCE

Half Marathon:13.1 miles

Marathon:26.2 miles

Triathlon: Swim, Bike, Run

Olympic:(0.93 mile swim, 24.85 mile bike, 6.2 mile run)

IRONMAN® 70.3 triathlon: Half distance (1.2 mile swim, 56 mile bike, 13.1 mile run)

***Full-distance IRONMAN® triathlon:**140.6 miles (2.4 mile swim, 112 mile bike, 26.2 mile run)

Ultra Run:26.2 miles +

*IRONMAN® events: The 140.6 distance began in Hawaii, 18th February 1978 by Judy & John Collins who began the race to determine who was the better athlete, swimmer, cyclist or runner.

ROCKY FILENAME	
iROCKY Michael Bibb	
OCCUPATION	Coach Author
MADE THEIR ENTRANCE	26th June 1970 Coventry, UK
EDUCATION	Sidney Stringer (Coventry) Guildhall Of Music & Drama/City University (London)
AKA	Rocky iRocky
ACHIEVEMENTS	This books charts some of his adventures

Who is this voice? Who is this bloke? Why should we listen to you? Fair questions all, let's start at the beginning. I was born to Naomi – everyone calls her Penny (there is another book right there, for now let me say thanks for being one of my heroes Mum!) – in the summer of 1970. I was raised by her, and her parents Frank and Kit, in council housing. We had very little but the beauty, looking back, was that we wanted for very little too. I never excelled at any sport at school – unless you include chess. I was the fat kid who, one wet lunchtime, rocked up at school chess club and got a place on the team shortly after; it turned out I did have a talent. Before the age of 20, I had chalked up a number of nondescript jobs: first at the local Working Men's Club (age 12), paperboy... you get the idea. I am working class in full effect, and I'm mentioning this because this is part of my story, just as your background has affected and affects you and what you do, and how you work/look at the world now.

I ran a bar for a while, found myself fascinated with people, took my first acting job with a touring theatre company at the age of 19, then worked an office job whilst auditioning for drama school – that goal was achieved in 1992. I went to the Guildhall School of Music and Drama and loved it – I had my shot at living my "Dream." I'm telling you all this now, so you know there was no silver spoon, the path of one's life does take us to some colourful places and this was the start of my journey, but it didn't reveal what would be coming up – I had no idea – it was impossible...

My wish is that you will be inspired to do something that you hitherto thought impossible through our travels together. You will go to some places, some will be exhilarating to visit, some excruciating, the throughline here is to inform through experience, so that your experience of life is as full as you want it to be. The aim is that when you picture that older version of yourself, that person will be defined by the actions that you took, deliberate actions, on your terms, carving that older self of yours – own it. You will hear of struggles, in fact you could argue that life is all about struggles, that it is what gives us meaning and what defines us.

....

MEETING YOUR CHIMP

You might know this already, you might not, but you have an animal inside you. It was born when you were born, it tries to protect you by chattering in your head. Yes, I hate to break it to you if this has escaped you, but you have a chimp inside your own head! Let's try to pull the chimp out of the hat to demonstrate. I was first introduced to "the chimp," by Sir David Brailsford CBE (former head of British Cycling). He was fresh back from the Team GB Olympic win in Beijing in 2008. He spoke to us about the huge success they had with their medal hoard in China and shared some of the secrets of their success. The team worked with Professor Steve Peters, sports psychologist (who later published his work/findings in The Chimp Paradox). All their cyclists had to believe that they were podium material and had to demonstrate it to make and stay in the team. Brailsford shared that one of the cyclists used to cry, another used to get very physical after a training set in frustration – this behaviour wasn't getting them across the race line any quicker and that was what being with Team GB was all about. Winning medals was the goal and any behaviour moving away from that goal was the chimp showing itself and had to be stopped.

First off though, they had to identify when the chimp had come out of the box, so to speak, by recognising this unwanted unproductive behaviour. They were then able to not react emotionally, as they had in the past, and acknowledge "Ah, that's just my chimp talking," and continue uninterrupted in the positive development of their craft. They could get on with their job and focus on the inch by inch small steps, the one per cent improvements, and not get derailed by that emotional, irrational side of us that isn't focused on the goal. NO DRAMA!

They became so focused that they even got specialists in to teach them how to wash their hands properly, because they wanted to avoid any illness or sick days as this would impact their training. Any days off were taking them further away from the gold medal! So if professional athletes had to stand in front of a sink with some soap and water for the greater good, just go with me to our MUSEum and keep the mind open, and not blocked by your chimp or some King Kong-style mind block.

Do you know the signs in yourself when your chimp makes its presence known? We will look at superhero thinking later, but this is the opposite. When your chimp comes out of the box, this is your emotive, less rational side showing its face; it is the unadulterated HULK side with no control or problem-solving skill. A tantrum, a capitulation to failure, a strop, the critic, the 'can-do' side of you is quiet and all the obstacles look insurmountable. You know what this looks and feels like when this happens. However, the key is to identify the habits you have when your chimp is *about* to show its face. You will never silence your chimp, but you can control the volume.

Your chimp will be telling you right now to dismiss this, that this is all nonsense, a couple of sports aces, artsy folk and a scientist, what? Museum, muse, meditation, there is no Museum of the mind, it's silly! He's talking about magic but you've seen magicians before, you know how it works – the rabbit is always there – there is no magic. Move on.

Look around you: gravity, empathy/love, how were the Pyramids built? These are all magic wonders that we take for granted everyday, but they are real anomalies and science cannot truly explain them away, yet we conveniently just brush them under the carpet and say, "It was the big bang," – again a theory. Bigger than that, science cannot explain why there is a universe and why there is life, and what it's all about. But we go about our day-to-day lives and gravity continues to stick us here (the weaker of the other universal forces and bettered by a simple fridge magnet) and the formation of some blocks in Giza in line with the constellation of Orion – a structure unable to be recreated today and built some 5,000 years ago (science thinks) – is a constant reminder that life is a mystery and that we don't know everything. So let us agree there is a lot of stuff out there that we just don't have a scooby doo about. By setting these boundaries we agree that magic happens, or at least there is a lot of stuff that happens that is impossible, but it happens anyway.

. . . .

WHAT IS MAGIC?

Magic; the power of apparently influencing events by using mysterious or supernatural forces.

. . . .

> "I want to be an idea, I want to represent possibilities, I want to represent magic, right? ... Like make a choice. You just decide what it's gonna be, who you're gonna be, how you're gonna do it. You just decide." Will Smith[3]

Thanks Will — it is not my place to convert you to the magic circle (I'm not a member myself). What is important though is to suspend our cynical, know it all, 21st century attitude, because quite simply we don't know it all. Darwinism is the *theory* of evolution, Newton was a very clever chap and then

[3] Speech by Will Smith, Goalcast, 30 June 2016, available at: www.facebook. com/watch/?v=1053041381439718

Einstein came along to trump him with his *theory* of relativity, and then dark matter came along and put a hole in Einstein's *theory* – but that is all they are: *Theories*... So, when your chimp decides to butt in and say that it is impossible, or it limits you, or it is being a critic, just say right back, "Gravity" or "Pyramids" or "Dark matter." Silence the chimp and move on. You don't have to believe in magic per se, but you do need to feel the goosebump moments or, at the very least, feel that carpet that you conveniently brushed a lot of stuff under as it starts to move underneath you.

Therefore, if a single mum can work her way to win her second Nobel prize, if a father and quadriplegic son can complete an IRONMAN® race, if a cancer sufferer is able to cycle from John O'Groats to Lands End and stop in for her chemo treatments along the way, if people aged 100+ years are creating new indoor cycling records or jumping out of planes, if a sports team (from a tiny island in the Pacific) can hold a winning average of over 80 per cent in their sport for over 100 years, if a boxer can say with absolute conviction that he is the greatest even before having a shot at the heavyweight title, if I can go Ultra and take on the Sahara – it must be magic, if not then what?

. . . .

BE PART OF THE R.O.C.K.Y PROJECT

In this book, I have included life-sized and epic inspirations, and mentors. They each cut a path to greatness in their own way, overcoming adversity and challenges on the way. The world, in their time, was telling them that they couldn't do something, but they did it anyway. They learned from their struggles, making themselves and the world richer in the process.

I pray you find your riches, wherever they lie. If being the best father you can be for your family is true wealth, I hope you are it. If your career is that lost island you sail across oceans to find, I hope you land safely. Be inspired, see your destination, take that inspiration as your fuel and then use your next chapter to inspire others to reach their destination. This is surely the way greatness lies.

The R.O.C.K.Y Project is a companion for your journey with some fellow travellers to help you some of the way. They have been where you are right now and decided there was more, that they could be more and that they could achieve more.

CHAPTER 1:
JOURNEY

DAVID GOGGINS

. . . .

"From the time you take your first breath, you become eligible to die. You also become eligible to find your greatness and become the One Warrior. But it is up to you to equip yourself for the battle ahead."

David Goggins[4]

[4] David Goggins, (2018), 'Can't Hurt Me: Master Your Mind and Defy the Odds', *Lioncrest Publishing*

Journey, a long and often difficult process of personal change and development.

. . . .

To help us explore 'Journey', the first ambassador I am going to introduce you to has also cited Rocky as a personal inspiration.

As I write an introduction for our first case study, I am smiling. I had to go all the way to Miami for a financial services seminar to learn about David Goggins, somewhat ironically, from a guy from my own county in the UK. MT introduced me to David Goggins at the Million Dollar Round Table (MDRT) annual gathering in 2019, with his memorable line of "You've read Can't Hurt Me, right?" That was the moment I became aware of this relentless force of nature. His self-published book details his brutal childhood, his bullied teenage years and he articulates what a lost soul he was and then, without wishing to sound over-the-top, the man becomes a true phoenix rising from the ashes; many superlatives have been thrown at him but in essence he is this grit-filled, mind mastery, one-in-a-million man.

What he does for me is get me to challenge myself and carry on when I feel I don't have anything else. I do feel that we are kindred spirits as he too had an epiphany when watching Rocky (I) – he calls it his "taking souls" moment. For him, it came in the 14th round after Apollo has knocked Rocky down and thinks it's all over. Picture the scene: Apollo goes to his corner and starts to prematurely celebrate; Rocky is being counted out but gets back up to beat the count. Apollo sees him rise and realises that the blistering fight will continue. In that moment, he knows that Rocky will not go down and stay down. Apollo drops his celebratory arms, his head drops too and he shakes his head in disbelief, admitting that he cannot beat Rocky, recognising him as a force of nature; Rocky has indeed "taken his soul." Goggins talks about how that scene stayed with him and how he uses it to get into people's minds, whether on Hell Week (Navy Seal training) or one of the many, many challenges that he has either thrown himself into, or that life has thrown at him.

This enduring feat of just keeping going is embedded in a famous Japanese proverb, "Fall down seven times, get up eight," you pick yourself up. Rocky, and Goggins, embodies this and that is what I hope comes across to you in this book – your fight is not finished, you are not done yet. I am not talking about putting on boxing gloves, but Goggins, Wright, Curie, Hoyt and all our featured case studies, have all kept going. They haven't given up when others might have counted them out. We all have our own fight be it a dream/goal career, relationships, day-to-day activities or leaving a legacy. So, I ask you again (and it will not be for the last time): What will your legacy be? Let us start in the present to inform the future and what better ambassador than Goggins. He can be likened to a modern-day Gladiator but in the world's colosseum. All I can say is, "Goggins we salute you."

ROCKY FILENAME

Goggins
David Goggins

OCCUPATION	United States Navy SEAL and former United States Air Force Tactical Air Control (RETIRED) Ultramarathon Runner, Triathlete/ Ultraman (an Ultraman is 6.2 mile swim, a 261.4 mile bike ride and a 52.4 mile run) Author of Can't Hurt Me: Master Your Mind and Defy the Odds Former Pull Up World Record Holder Motivational Speaker (Motivational fullstop!)
MADE THEIR ENTRANCE	17th February, 1975 Buffalo, New York, US Charity
EDUCATION	Ranger School "Top Honor Man" Military 1994 US Air Force Tactical Air Control Party (TACP) 2001 Navy SEAL 2004 Army Ranger
AKA	Toughest Man in the World Can't Hurt Me (CHM)
ACHIEVEMENTS	2005 Began ultra running to raise funds for The Special Operations Warrior Foundation. He competed in 24-hour ultra runs, Badwater 135, and the Ultraman World Championships.

Goggins and his Mum had to escape his abusive and violent Dad to survive. He cheated his way through school because of learning difficulties, and it was at his lowest point, when he was working as a pest exterminator, that he happened to see a documentary on Basic Underwater Demolition (BUDS/ Navy SEAL training). To say that he was out of shape at this point in his life is an understatement. He was carrying 'a lot of timber' at the time, too much for him even to be considered, which meant he had to lose a massive amount of weight in a short amount of time.

Remarkably, he lost the weight but just when the end was in sight, he got injured and had to do it all again. This then happened *again* – check out BUDS/Hell Week to gauge the level of disappointment for yourself. Just imagine going through all that pain and anguish, seeing the finishing line and then having to go back to day one, not just once but three times. Lesser men would have walked away, but not Goggins. This is just the start of his forging in the fire and in doing so, he got to inspire the world, not to mention all the money he has raised for charity. He also became an accidental ultra runner and has faced many physical challenges, oftentimes in spite of injury or experience. Goggins does not try, he simply does.

Not obstacles, this man has mountains in front of him: asthma, obesity (before deciding to step up to the plate for the US Navy SEAL), heart defect (detected 2010). That's not even including all the bits of his body he has broken during his runs and he has even experienced organ failure. I share this to point out that he is not a perfect physical specimen and has faced many physical setbacks – so let us be real about what an obstacle is, shall we. Even to this day, after shedding all the pounds, he says that his fat guy is still inside him and saying, "feed me."

We will recognise the chimp inside of all of us anon, but it is refreshing to hear from Goggins that it is not easy for him either. He has to keep working at it and like all of us, he too "hears the voices." What is your resolve? What will help you quieten down the 'fat you', the 'I want to quit' you? We all need a defence, a stronger voice to turn the volume down on the chimp.

He has completed three Navy SEAL Hell Weeks, run 100 miles in 19 hours as a complete rookie and has gone on to do Moab 240 and other ultra runs, has done over 4,000 pull-ups in 24 hours (a former Guinness World Record), and completed the IRONMAN® World Championships in just over 11 hours. This is a truly impressive list of endurance achievements and we could go on, and on. Ironically, he himself says, *"Nobody cares what you did yesterday. What have you done today to better yourself?"*

. . . .

THE HERO'S JOURNEY (JOSEPH CAMPBELL)[5]

Joseph Campbell was fascinated by world myths. He noticed over his many years of research that there were common themes from the East to the West – where there was no cultural crossover the myths at the heart of each culture were the same, with the same ingredients and same narrative – he called his discovery the Hero's Journey. In it, he outlined the steps, the landmarks, on the journey. They will be familiar as they are the path for most of the movies you have ever seen:

1. The Ordinary World
2. The Call to Adventure
3. Refusal of the Call
4. Meeting with the Mentor
5. Crossing the Threshold to the Special World
6. Tests, Allies and Enemies
7. Approach to the Innermost Cave
8. The Ordeal
9. The Reward
10. The Road Back
11. The Resurrection
12. Return with the Elixir

[5] Joseph Campbell, (2014), *The Hero's Journey: Joseph Campbell on His Life and Work,* New World Library, 3rd edition

Do any of these look familiar? Have you ever been on the threshold? Did you stay at point three?

Does it really need to be otherworldly? For example – imagine a boy who wants to be a doctor, but gets told that he isn't clever enough and so he stays in that ordinary world, and stops questioning his potential. He wasn't trained up and so he wasn't there on that night at A&E when a patient came in; he couldn't use his skill to save the patient. This has a knock on effect for the patient's family and perhaps some who now will not be born, and bring their skills to the world. However, he could have performed his hero role, perhaps after meeting his inspirational mentor at medical school and crossing the threshold into what it means to be a healer, working super-human hours on little sustenance and little sleep, saving lives, using his gifts and becoming that powerful force of nature EVERYDAY. However, the world never knew him or benefitted from his skill because he didn't answer the call. There is enough ordinary in this world – as we move forward, let this be the time of everyday heroes hearing the call – of doing what you were born to do and encouraging others to do so.

So let us look at the David Goggins' journey running through Campbell's Hero's Journey 12 steps template:

1. ORDINARY WORLD

Goggins the 'exterminator', clinically obese, existing, that is all, clocking in and clocking out; sound familiar?

2. CALL TO ADVENTURE

He accidentally watches Hell Week and this is his call to action. He knew the path that he was walking was going to lead to a shortened life expectancy. Seeing what those inductees were going through, their pain, their grit, their will to endure, awoke something in him and disturbed him enough to change his course and start his journey.

3. REFUSAL OF THE CALL

To this point he had tried previously to find a unit, a purpose, but when told that he had to retake the Pararescue he refused it and turned his back on his destiny.

4. MEETING THE MENTOR

Too overweight to be considered and getting many push backs or outright rejections, he keeps knocking on doors until he meets the one recruiting officer who gives him the solution – lose the many pounds within weeks – an impossible feat (?) – and we'll give you a shot. He takes up the opportunity.

5. CROSSING THE THRESHOLD

He changes his lifestyle/mindset, loses the pounds and proves he has the stuff. He makes it into the arena, he is on Navy Seal training!

6. TESTS, ALLIES, ENEMIES

He is tested and tested and tested. He faces the same challenges as he did with the Pararescue training and his injuries start mounting up, putting his goal further from reach. He becomes his own worst enemy and only passes training on the third attempt. He overcomes and learns that it is about HIM against HIM. There might be haters out there, there always will be, but the lesson is that it is YOU against YOU. You are your own worst enemy, far worse than anyone else out there. You decide what you can and can't do. Goggins begins not only chiselling his body but also his mind.

7. APPROACH TO THE INMOST CAVE

Not satisfied with completing arguably one of the hardest training programs (three times), he decides to go for Ranger School.

8. ORDEAL

Goggins serves in the Middle East/Discovers he has a hole in his heart and needs corrective surgery/Broken bones ... the list goes on...

9. REWARD (SEIZING THE SWORD)

Goggins is decorated for his efforts (let us remember that he was the big exterminator guy – going from restaurant to restaurant in the early mornings, clearing out rats and cockroaches – that was his life, does this sound like a real journey to you?).

10. THE ROAD BACK

His Hero's Journey is not yet over; now comes his higher cause and this is a direct impact of the loss of several of his colleagues, who were killed in action. Goggins takes up the cause to raise money for their children's college education and this is how Goggins the endurance athlete is born. He decides to make Badwater 135 his holy grail, but first he has to run a 100-mile race to prove himself (once again) for entry to Badwater. Armed with a deck chair, some crackers and Gatorade, breaking several bones in his feet and his body shutting down on him, he makes the 100 miles, gets his ticket to Badwater and begins raising millions of dollars for lost servicemen's/women's children.

11. RESURRECTION

We see Goggins time and time again taking on feats, such as the world record challenge, ultra events, Ultraman, Moab 240 (yep, running 240 miles). He throws himself at the world, like a piece of marble trying to define itself with its constant impact of throwing itself on the hard rock again and again, will it break or will it just become more defined?

12. RETURN WITH THE ELIXIR

The last stage of the Hero's Journey. The Hero returns, but he is not the same Goggins as he was at Stage 1. Growth has been exponential, achievements once unthought of, now firmly under his belt. He is indeed an "uncommon man" who has done and will continue to do uncommon things. The elixir is himself, his "Accountability Mirror." If he can go on this journey, with the 100s of extra pounds in weight he carried for years, the injuries, the asthma, sickle-cell anaemia, a heart defect; if he can, then brothers and sisters look to what is holding you back from your dreams and making them just another stage in your Hero's Journey. Do not settle, do not give up. Goggins' treasure, his gift to us, is that if HE can, then so can YOU!

So which Goggins are you then? Where are you on the journey? If we flip to film, which Neo are you? Matrix or Matrix

Revolutions? Or are you still that same old Mr Anderson with no idea of your potential, living but only going through the motions and waiting to be woken up? Which Luke Skywalker are you? Episode IV or Episode VII? Farm boy, or the last Jedi? Which Rocky are you? Rocky I or Rocky Balboa or, for those who aren't fans of the movies and wished they'd never bought this book, which version of you are you right now, at this moment?

There are many versions of you, of Jedi's in training, of Rocky's struggling to get into the ring for the fight that is worth fighting. What are you passionate about? What is your good fight and what are you doing about it, or have you let it go? Are you someone who has the eye of the tiger or someone who feels that they live in the eye of the storm, with no control over your life and the potential that was once so present, buried deep?

For full disclosure, I still see myself as Luke Skywalker in Episode IV: A New Hope, someone finding himself and with each challenge/obstacle/setback becoming more defined. He is on a quest, he sets out, the world is wide and he is still learning. Where are we on our journey? If we follow Luke's journey to the latest chapter in the saga (spoiler alert), he is a footnote, a haggard, bearded old man who has lost his way. My point is, you choose. You are the hero of your story, whether you like it or not. It doesn't matter whether you are East or West, mechanic, artist, builder, shop assistant, CEO or you sell life assurance for a living – you are "the one" in your life. You are the Jedi, you are the boxer taking on the fight of your life, you are with you 24/7; so decide if you are a passenger or if you are going to take the wheel.

Let's take this a stage further, for fun, have you come across superhero thinking? Well, with the advent of Marvel comic books taking over the movies from Avengers to Deadpool, and DC with Batman to Justice League, naturally these more-than-human individuals are in our psyche now more than ever. Ask yourself how would Superman solve this problem? And yes, you may go straight for the laser from the eyes, or the power of flight, but play with it and see where it takes you.

For example, let's say you have a really busy day lined up, with lots of appointments. In short, your day is hectic. How would Superman handle a similar day? You could say he would fly to each meeting and he's so fast it wouldn't be a problem for him. True, I can't argue with your logic, but this is about you using superhero thinking not donning tights and launching off rooftops. Just go with me on this for a moment, let's look at how we could make this a non-problem for you. As far as I am aware, none of my readers hail from the planet Krypton so let's say that you can't fly, but Superman has already solved the problem for you. Speed is the key or rather travelling fleet of foot, so make your appointments close together, or even in the same room, and just do one appointment with all the attendees (dependent on your business and the service you offer). If you have to travel, is it worth getting a driver, so you can focus on your next meeting instead of listening to the Sat Nav and getting infected by road rage? Or could you catch a train or a plane and prep, and focus, for the meeting. From impossible to possible – thank you Marvel and DC.

I'll share another example just to bring this home. Let's say you have a challenging relationship, a work colleague, family, friend, your call; now let's be outrageous with this and take it to extremes. You have a communication/relationship issue – how would Wonder Woman solve this? Give yourself a minute...

Yes she would get to the truth, she would get right to the heart of it. Easy for her, I hear you say. She has that magic rope (the Lasso of Truth) and that is true too, but the point is she aims for the truth. Truth can always be your weapon too, you have words, thoughts and actions – these are your tools and you can achieve the same end.

How would The Hulk deal with a bad day? Do you ever get bad days? What wisdom could Marvel reveal to us with some superhero thinking?

Now you just saw The Hulk get angry didn't you? And yes, that is an option. The Hulk gets angry and smashes things, *but* The Hulk is also Bruce Banner the scientist with multiple PHDs and he chooses when to get angry (at least that's what he tells us in Avengers), so choose not to get angry. Choose to be the rational Bruce Banner who knows the consequences of "going green." Use the brain instead of the strong arm; might that help? Now you can see where this outrageous superhero thinking can help you solve problems.

One more for good measure, but this time with Rocky, just to demonstrate that by taking this to the zenith, there is a gift here for you. Can we talk about success? Let us agree that success isn't just about having millions in the bank. Success is having a happy, healthy, meaningful life – your bank balance just gives you choices. As far as I am aware, no one has ever been on their deathbed and asked for the latest balance in their current account. Success is about leading a significant life.

You no doubt have your own picture of success, your own ideal/target, let's say that it is to get a promotion, or exercise more? How would Rocky solve this? Rocky is not a superhero, but a boxer, how could he make it work? Work it through, he would get a good coach in his corner, someone that believes in him. He would work hard, he would work harder than anyone else in the room, because that is his work ethic, (as an aside the legendary Olympian Sir Steve Redgrave, when asked the secret of his success, says that he was the only one out rowing on Christmas day), and he would probably ask his closest friends and family to help him.

**EXERCISE TIME:
SUPERHERO SLO-MO**

For fun (as your brain is probably hurting), get up slowly, slo-mo style, lead with the head, when at your full height with fists clenched, rest them on your hips and look to the distance on the left, hold that pose. Sit down, repeat and once more with feeling, hold that pose with your chin slightly raised. Then say, "I am going to do great things!"

How do you feel? Empowering isn't? This is a great tool to re-energise and at the very least, laugh at yourself (in a good way) and shake off some of the cobwebs. Play with it, find your own signature move and have some fun. Get your kids involved – what does their 'super' move look like?

Coming back to you, as the hero of your days and for any doubting Thomas's out there, this is undeniable. You are the protagonist of your own story. You are the hero that has your own quest. This could be to have a quiet life, this could be to have a larger-than-life life BUT this is your life, you decide to make the calls, you decide to get into the car, you decide on your car, your home, your family.

Why using The R.O.C.K.Y Project works well is that we do need to have a reality check of our own. We get so involved in other's stories that oftentimes it can be sometime before we revisit our own journey and that of our own household heroes such as our children, partners and parents. Having something, or someone, outside of ourselves acts as a wake up call, especially when you ask yourself what have I done for them recently? What good have I done today for my team? Rocky is a man of the people and for the people, he never forgot where he came from, he had a strong work ethic and always came back to his origins.

If this book was just about superhero types like Goggins you could be excused for thinking, "Well that isn't about me, he is a different mould." There is no respite for you though, as we are all from a different mould and included here are some of the episodes in my Hero's Journey as that everyman character, clinically obese, with not much time to train due to family commitments, but isn't that the same for all of us?

....

iROCKY

WHAT ARE YOU WAITING FOR?

In 1998, this author decided to "do life." I was fed up of waiting for that break, where someone else is deciding on, or determining, my fate. "Doing life" meant getting a "proper" job, something reliable and dependable, if I wanted to get a mortgage, buy a house and start making a family of my own. As I write this book, let me add, never aspire to have a mortgage or if you do, then equally aspire to pay it off early! All part of being clear about your dreams and visualising specifically where you want to be – always ensure that wherever you are, whatever you're doing is debt free – this is freedom and being here at 50 is a beautiful view, I went the long way around but have got here.

The "proper" job was in financial services, and my apprentice-ship in this field still continues, a keynote change was when I took the lessons to date and started my own practice in 2007. This wasn't just about wealth management, it was about peo-ple's lives. I was able to take what I learned through my training and the hard knocks of being self-employed, to define what I was self-employed to do and that was/is encourage those I work with to write their own lives, be it financial freedom, retiring happy, passing on their legacy to the next generation, having peace of mind, or just encouraging them to follow their dreams. I then understood my place. My role on this Earth, put simply, is to help people, not to direct but collaborate, not to judge but to listen, to encourage, to help make a life or, as you will read, sometimes even save a life or two. Clients now are friends, I am deeply involved in their story and the money is just there to give them the life they want.

It is equally important to add that after putting down roots and wanting a family, I've been married for 20+ years and we are still on the dance floor. We have four children who constantly keep us working on balance: on being a Dad, Hus-band, business owner and, dare I say, albeit with a small "a" (a very small "a"), an athlete. This introduction is important as you are investing your precious time to read these words and by hearing my story, it will add currency to what comes next.

I mentioned the word athlete but really do need to position this too. Over the last few years I have surprised myself with some of the challenges I have chalked up and it is through mindset and dreaming big that I have endured, BUT let us be clear! – I'm a back of the pack athlete, with minimal training, and I cannot see myself ever winning any of these challenges, but that is not my why. Balance is all, I commit to my training as I do my family and business; for me it has never been about hedonistically throwing myself into a program where I don't see my wife and kids, and client relationships suffer because it is all about me, my ego and chasing my PB; that has never been my thing. In our Muse, and for the purposes of your journey 'The MUSEum', I work constantly on mental strength and it is this that perhaps has a gift for you in its hands. Endurance means to keep going, it means to suffer it and for you to keep going when others have stopped. This life business is not about the destination, about how big your house is, about what car you drive, about your job title, it is all about the journey, your journey and to keep going.

Why use sport/triathlon experience? Simply because I am the most unlikely candidate. It is a vehicle of the possible, like how the honey bee keeps flying, how a movie about a failed Olympic ski jumper can uplift and inspire. The wonder is in striving and resilience. For the purposes of your time here, see me as the Eddie the Eagle of triathlon. My endeavours are not those of Ernest Shackleton or Ranulph Fiennes, Sherpa Tenzing

Norgay or Nelson Mandela. Mine is the story of an everyman who is still living the life of an everyman, feet on the ground but reaching for the stars. Whether your thing is sport, art, science, business or being the best Dad/Mum you can be, decide on your vehicle, your channel and rage against the possible. It is the daring that counts, and the reaching.

. . . .

LONDON MARATHON, 2000 (SUPPOSED TO BE MY FIRST AND LAST MARATHON!)

At 30, my thinking was that I knew I had a marathon in me and wanted to get it done before I got too old. I got a charity spot with Rainbow Trust, bleached my hair and all such to raise funds for them. Naivety or youth, I went out running from scratch about ten times only, in the last weeks of the build up to the April start. On my first last big run (over 15 miles) on the build up to London, at around mile 18 one of the biggest lessons hit me and has stayed with me to this day. I was heading home, but in my head, I knew these hills were coming and yet I kept going, and going. The hills were getting closer and then I just stopped running, but I was smiling – I was smiling because I knew that my body could keep going, it was my head that said no. I smiled because I knew I could go the distance. The lesson was: manage the mind and the body will follow. Up to that point I hadn't given that a thought – to be fair, other than thinking I had to chalk up some runs I hadn't given the whole venture much thought, all I needed was an old pair of Nike's, a pair of shorts and a T-shirt and we are good to go.

In that respect I was similar to Goggins, (well not quite), he just rocked up for his first ultra run, a 24-hour race, his mission to chalk up 100 miles, to be fair though he did have a deck chair and a drink with him! Perhaps all those years of not being a runner had bottled up in me – it felt great to be in London with the crowd willing you on every step of the way. Not much to report back on this one – it was clinical, a bucket list item, checked off, time was sub 4:30 but I really wasn't chasing a time, I just wanted to chalk it up. Little did I know that 17 years later I would be running a marathon after a 2.4-mile swim and a 112-mile bike.

If you had time travelled back to me then and told me that I would even be contemplating that distance, I would have laughed you all the way down The Mall. That would be impossible, as I couldn't really swim, I was never a cyclist and I had done a marathon, and that was enough. And yet here we are. What changed? What moved the goalposts from 26.2 miles to 140.6 miles? This life business is amazing if you just live with purpose, and instead of saying, "Not for me" try saying, "Why not for me?" it will take you to places you never thought you'd get to. Allow yourself to be that time traveller, go back to yourself "back in the day" and think about what you had achieved, and thought that was that (e.g. marathon or A-levels, degree, business startup, starting a family). Look how far you have come and if you have that road not taken allow yourself to begin that journey, no matter how long ago or how far away it feels.

Artist Carmen Herrera (106 years old in 2021) had her only major show back in 1984 and then in 2016: the Whitney Museum (yes that Museum word has come up again!) gave her solo gallery shows, she was 101 years old. That's a 32 year wait. That is some journey from producing art in her 50s, to being celebrated as an Art Hero as a centenarian.

What is your Hero's Journey? What is your nearest and dearest's Hero's Journey? What is your colleague's/client's Hero's Journey? We cannot only look to the ancient myths, such as Jason and his argonauts, Achilles and Hercules for the inspiration, but rather as a map for us or like Ali holding up the torch to light our way, a sign post: HEROES THIS WAY AND LARGE ARROW.

We all have our own challenges, that undiscovered country, that "us" that we always wanted to be, that deed we always wanted to do. Are you a Luke Skywalker or are you an Obi-Wan? Where are you? Are you mentoring/teaching others without knowing it? That first day at school, that inspirational teacher, that opportunity of a lifetime... Are you seizing it? Are you a mentor, encouraging and coaching others to go for it?

How often do we ask, how can I help you? Being of service, or having a mission or quest is what defines us, so don't just wait at the port watching the ships returning and leaving, get on one. This little gem began with a bicycle, but we still had to make that boat...

....

LONDON TO ROME
(MMXII-MMXV) 2012-2015

When we talk of marathons, or extreme challenges, it is easy to think, "I want to be the first one across the line," maybe it is because of my attitude or the way I am built physically. I have the build and frame of Eddie Izzard and, like Eddie, I was a late bloomer to sport but like Eddie too, it is my attitude that defines me. Like him, I signed up for some stuff and was surprised at what I had in me and that I could keep going. In my next book, Eddie will feature as, I don't know about you, but watching his 2009 marathon-a-day run through the UK (some 43 marathons in 51 days) he challenged us all to check in with what is possible and became a torch bearer of "If I can, you can." It was at Crieff Hydro, Hogmanay 2011, that I was asked to join The London to Paris cycle, from the O2 Arena to the Eiffel Tower. I didn't even have a road bike, it had been 20 years since I sat on a bike with a destination in mind, BUT it was for charity and it was Hogmanay and a couple of glasses of wine had been imbibed... I signed up.

Using our time travel journeying, if you would have told me, as we waited at the O2 to pedal off, that at the drinks stop on that very first day (with the added time pressure of the Olympic

Torch coming into Dover) I would cycle back up route to relieve one of the team who had been helping my little cousin (he had had no less than four punctures), I would have laughed you out of the O2 car park. The road closures in Dover were a real problem and we were told that if we didn't get to the port by a certain time we wouldn't see France. Most of the team waited at the last drinks stop, the marshalls were starting to pack up, when I said the following, "You guys are getting cold, you carry on and I will go back and tag Jason." At the time, I didn't fully appreciate that this was my Rocky revealing himself. I was not the best cyclist and am still not, but this was like a call to arms for me. I wouldn't be the first one, but I was born to make sure we all get across the line.

Cycling back I tagged in, so the other team mate could press on and get some nourishment and replenish his water bottles from the drink stop, as it was packing up and would soon be gone. The only real coach that I had had in my life to that point was Mickey (a la Rocky) and I used all the lines I could summon to get into my cousin's head. It was not pretty as he was in a bad place, getting one puncture is frustrating, two in the same day is unlucky – more than that in one day, and you feel cursed. His head was gone and he didn't want me to miss the rest of the tour, he was done.

Was it because I was focusing on someone else that I forgot about my own pain/fear of failing? Was it because he needed someone then, as his head was in a bad place, with all those punctures, or was it because I like helping people? Maybe all of the above, but what I do know is that many times he said something along the lines of, "leave me," "save yourself" etc and I stayed the course and told him he was doing this and, yes, even sang many tunes from Rocky, *No Easy Way Out*, *Eye of the Tiger*, *Going to Fly* – it made a difference. If it made a difference to two absolute amateurs on bikes, in the middle of nowhere, doing the hardest cycle they had ever done, with the weather and the Olympic Torch against them, then surely this can be applied to any situation.

I kid you not, as we endured and got into Dover I looked over my shoulder and saw the police were closing the road behind us. We got to the port and there was the rest of the team standing on the pavement, their anxiety for us turned to cheers as they spotted us and then shepherded Jason into the cafe to refuel, bring him back to life and celebrate phase one – complete.

Over the following days we travelled south through Northern France, we stopped at the Thiepval Memorial, a memorial to the lost/missing on the Somme. The sense of despair was palpable and when you see the photos of those whose destination is unknown, the faces of the youth – they were sons, brothers, lovers, husbands – gone, you couldn't help but look at our band of brothers and realise how fortunate we were to be here, "to be." This sense of gratitude, I would learn, is straight from the Stoics, most notably: Marcus Aurelius, Epictetus, Seneca, Zeno and Cato. It was here where I learned the value of stoicism, albeit by accident and it continues today to give me gratitude, and to keep challenging myself. It is only looking back on the tour that I remembered, ironically, that one of the team was affectionately called "Cato" (it was after Inspector Clouseau's sidekick from The Pink Panther movies, however I like to think the Stoics travelled and still travel with us, or at least their wisdom does).

We draw resilience, gratitude and humanity from the Stoics – theirs is a philosophy for happiness. The first real takeaway of theirs for you is "Amor fati" from the Latin, meaning to love one's fate. Good, bad and ugly we say thank you for what life gives us. The Stoics were stoicing around 2000 years ago and that might put some of you off, but Friedrich Nietzsche, during the 1880s wrote, "Amor fati: let that be my love henceforth! I do not want to wage war against what is ugly… some day I wish to be only a Yes-sayer."[6] Sounds good? Well, when we got to Paris it was the year that Bradley Wiggins had won the Tour and our mini-tour had arrived the day before, so we headed over to the Avenue des Champs-Élysées, the famous avenue in the 8th arrondissement of Paris, where the end of the Tour was coming in, to cheer Wiggins home! It looked like the whole of Paris had invested in some major sideburns and sported them, to honour his win. We found a bar and with the euphoria of our finish, and the Tour de France, coming in I was turning into a believer; I was turning into that Yes-sayer. "Let's not stop, let's keep going," I said, and over a couple of beers and with a map of Europe from the bartender we looked at our next leg. Having lived in Rome and loved the place I suggested that be our destination and, after considering that or Athens,

[6] Friedrich Nietzsche, Walter Kaufmann (translator), (1974), The Gay Science, Random House

we agreed on Rome. And so it was that we met the following year and picked up from the Eiffel Tower to Geneva, and then the next year onto Venice and then in 2015 we finally touched the Colosseum; our "Tour" was complete.

The point I am making here is that it could have all easily stopped if we hadn't made the ferry in time and beaten that Olympic Torch back in Dover, or if we had never said, "Yes" that Hogmanay in Crieff, BUT the following years proved that we could cycle across Europe to Rome. It was not the road not taken by us, but could have so easily been. In spite of no bike, and little experience, we managed to cross several countries, raising tens of thousands for charity because we said Yes. Amor fati – here endeth the lesson.

Well there's more where that came from, don't change that dial, let's see how Goggins fits within out Tour of R.O.C.K.Y:

. . . .

THE R.O.C.K.Y ROAD
FOR GOGGINS

Rise – This was a man who was beaten, obese and just existing. He was inspired by seeing a documentary about BUDS and the Navy Seals on TV, which gave him the push he needed to leave his life as an exterminator behind.

Obstacles – His head was willing but his body got broken, again and again.

Choices – He had a choice; to walk away and embrace his life as a guy who doesn't finish, or to rage against this. He comes back time and again, and it is through this mindset that he actually defines himself. It is through the trials and the suffering that Goggins is forged and his potential realised.

Kaizen – He then goes on to Ultra running and IRONMAN® races. In his first 100-mile race again his body breaks down, but he learnt that if your mind can live with it then so can your body. Even though he broke most of the small bones in his feet and had to get rushed to hospital, he did it. He then started asking himself, what else is possible? He worked on himself and became a world record holder.

You – Goggins' back was against the wall, he used everything he had to get through BUDS/Hell Week/Seal training. From the forge of failing, he gets back up again and again. He became known as one of the hardest men on the planet, a very far cry from his previous obese self. We all have this in us, the out of shape or the athletic You – you decide. Goggins had a mission that got him into running and this was to raise funds to pay for the education of his fallen comrades' children. What is your mission? What is the thing that will get you to your ideal version of you? Think about this and then choose: settle or strive.

. . . .

MUSEUM OF MOMENTUM TOUR

For our first foray into our MUSEum of Momentum we are going to focus on our first avatar, Goggins, from the perspective of journey. Picture a road going across the wall. At one end is Goggins as a big guy who loved big breakfasts, was working as a pest exterminator, and telling himself he was no good, a quitter. Then there is the moment he starts walking on that road and starts shedding not only the pounds but the negative, destructive thoughts. He writes a best-selling book, becomes an endurance athlete and earns kudos as one of the hardest men alive.

He has an amazing body, drive, will and grit, but we could have easily never heard of David Goggins. He could have slipped into obscurity, his potential never realised, trapped in a cave of his own design; his small apartment, filled with the trappings of mediocrity and reminders of how far he hadn't come. Even in these surroundings, he spotted his own spark for potential in the inductees in the BUDS/Navy Seals Hell Week on TV. Just like Michelangelo working on his 'David', he chipped away at a lump of marble, revealing his identity with each stroke. There was no shazam moment – it came through work, trials and with that calling, he began his journey in a truer sense.

So what is holding you back on your journey? Are you listening to that voice inside you that is telling you, you can do more, you can be more? Begin. Goggins, I grant you, is an extreme case. His determination and relentlessness puts him perhaps in a category of one. Isn't it infectious though? Aren't you wondering what is inside of you? Consider the place where he came from and where he is now – an obese pest exterminator driving down that same old dead-end road every day, to one of the most motivational and inspiring characters in the world. Do you have a mentor in your life? If not, why not? More on this anon, for now though, stand back from your life for a moment, survey the landscape you have traversed to get to this point, and the road, path or mountain pass you have travelled. Consider the struggles, the wins and all that you have had to overcome to get here. Do you like the view? Are you in a valley or atop a mountain? Is it enough? Can you rest?

EXERCISE TIME:
YOUR HERO'S JOURNEY

Take a moment and think about *your* Hero's Journey, looking at those identified 12 steps. Where are you? I am asking you both literally and figuratively, where are you? Is there something out there, calling you? It is okay if you haven't had that call to action yet – what's great about reading this book is that now, you will be more likely to take action when you hear the call.

If you're not sure where you are and would like some help figuring that out, I'm here for you. I love hearing about other people's journeys and would be honoured to support you on yours. I'll play the Mickey to your Rocky, just drop me a line at **therockyprojectexperience@gmail.com**

CHAPTER II

FAMILY

TEAM HOYT

. . . .

"When we first started running, I was getting calls and letters from people with disabilities that were very upset with me and they said I was just out there looking for glory and dragging my disabled son to all these races. They didn't know that it was him dragging his old man to these races."

Dick Hoyt

Family: a group consisting of one or two parents and their children.

....

"What's next now we've made it to The Colosseum? What's next?"

Silence.

"Let's do an IRONMAN® race!"

I am not the world's best swimmer, I only picked up the bike to do some charity cycles and I had never even heard of an IRONMAN® event. However, following our completion of the cycle to Rome, and keen to map out our next chapter, MC, JB (my cousin) and I met at Pizza Express, Shoreditch, in July 2015. I asked, "What is an IRONMAN® event?", MC shared the distances: a 2.4-mile swim, 112 miles on the bike and then a 26.2-mile run (140.6 miles in all). The swim is in open water, all thoughts of 'Amor fati' escaped me and my chimp brain, in spite of the Limoncello that MC had insisted adorn our table in honour of our Italian victory, was still freaking out. Then MC did something that was, and still is to this day, profound. He showed me the Team Hoyt film on YouTube (check it out and tell me you aren't swept away).

Inspiring is an understatement – if a father can swim across a lake, with a rope around his waist towing his adult son in a dinghy behind, I had no excuses. If Dick is swimming with

Rick in tow, there is no hiding place for me. As I watched the video, I thought if this man can swim for two, who am I to let something like poor technique/bad experience get in the way. I was inspired, I was tearful, I was "Hoyted" – like Shakespeare I am adding a new word to our language. Because of them I signed up for the IRONMAN® triathlon. This was in 2015, I could not really swim that far, I had cycled with the boys a little and my marathon was 15 years ago. Now this all has to be put together and done within 17 hours? "So what?" I hear you say (if you haven't checked them out on YouTube already, do it, it is a MUST). "They did a bit of swimming and Bibb, you're no good at swimming – so what?"

The Hoyts' story begins in 1962. Rick, due to oxygen depriva-tion to his brain prebirth became a victim of cerebral palsy, a quadraplegic. Rather than listening to the professionals of the day, who essentially told his parents, Dick and Judy Hoyt, to walk away; like true parents they decided then and there that they would stand the post and love their son and whatever the medical term or condition, that would not define him, he was their boy. They were not for turning their backs but embracing their youngest son and instead of walking away from him they found how to run WITH him.

Rick could not walk or speak but when the right technology came along from Tufts University, (akin to the device that Dr Stephen Hawking used), Rick found his voice. In 1977, Rick asked if he could do a five-mile benefit run for a lacrosse player who had been paralysed in an accident. Dick pushed Rick in his wheelchair; it was their first race but this was very much just the beginning. It was a revelation to them both and later that night, when Rick told his father, "Dad, when I'm running, it feels like I'm not disabled," Team Hoyt was born.

They have completed hundreds of races together, marathons (NB the Boston Marathon every year 1980-2014), duathlons and triathlons, including six IRONMAN® competitions (yes, you read that correctly!).

At the end of the 2.4-mile IRONMAN® triathlon swim, they have to exit the water (with no help from officials) and begin the 112-mile bike phase. Seeing Dick gently lift Rick out of the dinghy, (thanks to our friends at YouTube), then equally gently sit him in the special two-seater bicycle, you'll see Dick applying sun cream to his son and ensuring that his helmet is on comfortably. I know this is obvious stuff for a parent to do, but seeing them in motion is something else, it is a thing of beauty. For the last stage of the IRONMAN® triathlon, the 26.2-mile run, Dick then will push Rick in his bespoke running chair to the finish, where they're met by rapturous applause and elation. Just getting myself across the line seemed like my own Everest and here were the Hoyts doing it together, filling me with hope and determination.

ROCKY FILENAME	
TEAM HOYT Dick Hoyt & Rick Hoyt	
OCCUPATION	Physicist (DH) Researcher (Boston College – RH)
MADE THEIR ENTRANCE	(DH) 1st June 1940 Winchester, Massachusetts, US (RH) 10th January 1962 Holland, Massachusetts, US
TOOK THEIR LAST BOW	17th March 2021 (DH)
EDUCATION	Army & Air National Guard for 37 years (DH) Boston University (RH) Graduated 1993
AKA	Team Hoyt
ACHIEVEMENTS	Literally hundreds of races together, challenging limitations and opening the door for others to do something extraordinary that was previously thought impossible!

How do you measure greatness or achievement? What is impressive to you? Please take a moment to think about this as it will be a thread running throughout this book. We have all "done some stuff," and my humble stumblings are *nothing* compared to the Hoyts, in fact, compared to many. This is not false modesty, I have met and heard Olympians/Paralympians, world record holders, Everest climbers, adventurers and explorers, *they* have done some stuff – I am not looking for any dues. The challenges that I have taken on are inconsequential to many. That is not the point of this book though, the point is, it's not about me, it's about you and what you have done for yourself lately. What have you done for your family lately? Don't judge it, go with it, who should we compare ourselves to anyway? We each have our own obligations, our own trials and tribulations; our own hurdles and wings. What is a big deal to some is a molehill to others, but please think about your achievements, no matter how small. If you are brave enough, there will be room for you to write them down and acknowledge them in this book; after all this is *your* book so make it your own.

What further validated their place in my Hero Hall of Fame, was that whilst in Vancouver (June 2016) the whole Father's Day TV campaign/ad was centred around the boys of Team Hoyt and their togetherness, doggedness and just their wow factor for all that they had done.

What is this all for? What is it about? If it isn't for the family then what? For me it has to be all about them, my children. They are the reason, purpose and will tell my tale when I have shuffled off this mortal coil. More than that, from this point on they will be inspired to challenge themselves and climb their own mountains/goals and do their own marathons in life and when the going gets tough they can dig deep and keep going, even when they feel they have nothing left to give. If their old man can do marathons at 50 (God willing also at 60, 70 and beyond) then they can do this!

Team Hoyt inspires me. They are there, holding back the curtains and saying, "Go on, you've got this, if you want it."

. . . .

iROCKY

This might give you goosebumps – after seeing Team Hoyt and saying "yes" to IRONMAN® races some amazing things happened, very shortly afterwards:

1. I was offered a place for the London Marathon (2016)
2. I was offered a place for The London Triathlon (2016) and
3. I was offered a place for the Prudential London to Surrey 100 (2016)
   NB I did not apply for any of these, they came to me! Come on; who gets offered all these? It was as if I was getting help, or these were affirmations that I was taking the right road.

. . . .

THE LONDON MARATHON 2016

The highlights of the day were many, especially getting over-taken by folk who must have been in their 60s and were just cruising past me aged 45 (note to self, age is just an attitude), the crowd was always in my corner throughout the day cheering me on. I was running for the Rainbow Trust again so I was wearing their rainbow wig, their running vest and had added ROCKY to it, for some encouragement from the crowds. I wasn't disappointed, it felt like almost every other person who was leaning over the barriers was shouting "Rocky, Rocky, Rocky!", many others saw the name and burst into the Rocky theme! Thank you LONDON!

I was in some considerable pain for most of it, but as the man with the huge banner at the start of our race had chalked up: PAIN IS TEMPORARY – 26.2 LASTS FOREVER. It became spiritual in parts, seeing my children at the finishing line, seeing their smiles and seeing their faces, albeit in my mind's eye.

It got me thinking about the last time I did the London Marathon in 2000, when my friend Jim came to cheer me on, with Kevin and again with my chief cheerleader, my wife Pauline. Jim was one of the dubbed "Essex boys" (even though he came from Cornwall) and these boys all affectionately referred to each other as "loser". When he was standing on Tower Bridge around the halfway mark, I could see his big smile over the heads in the crowd and then he lifted a banner up to inspire me and of course, what else could it have had on there but the words "LOSER" in huge letters. In my mind's eye I saw Jim's face in the crowd a lot that day (more on Jim a little later). With three miles to go I was struggling as my right leg had decided it didn't want to participate after mile eight, when I saw a chap just walking, head down. Dennis was the name on his back, so I ran up to him and said, "Dennis you have got this, we are nearly there, come with me." I did this perhaps as much for myself as for him. He picked himself up and we ran shoulder to shoulder, all he kept saying was, "thank you", "thank you", which I have to say brought a few tears on for me. I didn't have much of a pace but it was enough to jump start him and we ran together, me saying words of encouragement (again for both our sakes), and Dennis saying thank you.

As we got closer to the finish, I could see that I was now holding him back, as my pace was impeded by my right stump! "Dennis, you are looking good – go for it," I said. He thanked me once more and off he went. I was now running a little faster knowing that I had made a difference and had to get myself across the line. Once I had finished, my right leg became almost mulelike and refused to go any further without a lot of persuasion, so I hobbled to the articulated lorry to get my kitbag, get warm and hopefully be reunited with my chief cheerleader, my wife Pauline. She was indeed waiting for me, with my pace now verging on slow motion (no hands on hips and raised chin looking distantly into the future, not this time), hands were being used to help move my legs, like a puppet with no strings. It took us a good 15 minutes to do a five-minute walk – my body was making it's protest known. Yes it was sore but it didn't last for long and that was one of the main takeaways from that day – it all passes and you only think of the achievement of doing something epic like a marathon. This is the "Yo I did it!" feeling, regardless of the obstacles/pain. At the back of my mind though I was thinking this was just a marathon, and if I am feeling like this now, how will I be next year after doing the 2.4-mile swim and 112-mile bike ride? My chimp was doing everything it could to get my attention and abort the IRONMAN® triathlon quest, but this journey that I was now set on meant that some serious development, nay a miracle, was required.

. . . .

THE PRUDENTIAL RIDE 100 LONDON – SURREY 31ST JULY 2016

This was to be my first planned 100-mile cycle. During our four-year bike bimble from London to Rome we had chalked up some century rides, but most were not intentional and with no clock against us (other than Dover before the Olympic torch and Geneva before the Tornado...). So, here I was ready to take it on and what a great way to get my mind prepared for the bigger cycle to come next year. The day swept by and finishing at Buckingham Palace was ace. Mission accomplished, I have done a marathon on foot, 100 miles on the bike (what's another 12?!) and onwards to The AJ Bell London Triathlon... and the swim Arrrrrrrrrrrrrrrrrghhhhhhhh!

. . . .

THE AJ BELL LONDON TRIATHLON 6TH AUGUST 2016 EXCEL LONDON

If the Prudential ride was uneventful for me, this triathlon was to be anything but. Just to remind you, at this point I could only do a very slow breaststroke, but for this event I had to swim 1.5k in the Thames, wetsuit, goggles and my heart racing like a rabbit petrified, almost paralysed, because the shadow of the hawk is flying overhead.

The river was like a judgement day for me and in many ways it became one. Now those of you who aren't confident swimmers, are probably thinking, "Rather you than me Guv," yep, I get it. What had I done? What had I signed up for? I knew no one there, I had never swum in the Thames and never swum with so many people – the race starts can be accurately described as a washing machine; I am sure you can picture it with all the competitors kicking off and thrashing away for their early head start. Truth be told I shouldn't have been there, or was it Kismet? Was I meant to be there, at that exact time, at that exact place – was I meant to be a poor swimmer at that time? Intrigued?

(Journal note Monday 8th August) Just had a call from the London Triathlon Medical Director to thank me and to let me know the competitor had collected his bike, bag/kit after recovering in hospital and he was tip-top. I said I was relieved to hear it, as he looked dead in the water and he said yes he may well have been if I hadn't taken action...

"You are a hero," I pushed back on that, he insisted, "You are, you bought us time."

You can't help but turn this stuff over inside your head. What I can't get away from is that I wouldn't have been in the water on Saturday if we hadn't started on the London to Rome journey, or if we hadn't met last July and decided to go on an IRONMAN® event journey together. I got a free entry only two weeks before to do this triathlon. I am a poor swimmer and even though I have the best intentions of doing the swim in front crawl, I do lose my bottle often and switch to breast stroke; as such, I was at the back pootling away.

Let me explain what happened. I jumped into the Thames by the Excel Arena for this Olympic-distance triathlon, only the sixth time in my wetsuit, and I was terrified. I was alone, everyone else had fired ahead. I soldiered on, then I heard a whistle. My first thought was, "shark!" (That's me the rabbit, prey, this is how the chimp makes us feel and it will use any pictures to get us away from the chimp's perceived danger). All the other swimmers were chasing a time, with their heads down powering through and couldn't hear the marshal's frantic whistling, but I was perfectly positioned to be there for him.

The marshal, in a small kayak, was haring towards me, whistle in mouth and blowing like crazy. I continued to swim, he stopped, and I realised there was a body, face down in the water. Due to it being an open water deep swim, one cannot touch the bottom and stand, the marshal is in a small kayak that's built for speed and therefore, he cannot pull the competitor out of the water entirely and help him, hence the whistle and hence me.

I got closer, by which point he had pulled the guy's head out of the water. The marshal then looked at me and said, "Emergency mouth-to-mouth now!" With one hand on the kayak and another on the stranger in the Thames, I tried to give the kiss of life, as best I could. I persevered and the competitor came to, but was in spasms and proceeded to bite my lip! By this time, other marshals had flocked to us and they were able to get the rest of his body out of the water straddling several of the small kayaks, and headed for shore. I was in the middle of the Thames, now bleeding, when a marshal kayaked over to me and said he would take me back. Instead of accepting the tow, I asked for a moment, composed myself and then continued the swim and race. For the rest of the race, I didn't know if the man I had helped had made it. I asked the marshals around the course on the run, they knew nothing and I have to say I did say more than a couple of "Our Fathers" and was praying for good news. I just wanted to finish the race as it was an exercise in, can I get through this? And as I was loaded up with this other competitor's plight, I was racing for two. That might sound odd to you, but it was tough and I had to keep going.

When I crossed the line, again I asked marshal after marshal for news, but nothing. I got back to the AJ Bell hospitality area, as I was their guest, and I asked our host if she knew anything about the chap in the water. The hospitality was on the second floor overlooking the river and she said, "Oh yes that was amazing, we were watching the race from the balcony, we saw the kayaks and a swimmer help him and then they got him out of the water." "That was me," I said and tears finally came, "I had to give him mouth-to-mouth, did he make it? Did he make it?" She could see I was choked and said she didn't know. Because I was bitten I had to report to one of the doctors'. They wanted me to go to hospital, but I said I had to get the train, so they wrote me a prescription and I had to see my GP, which resulted in a Hepatitis B jab for my trouble, but the day felt like a tsunami over me and I emerged from it, not a frightened rabbit anymore, but undefeated. If I could go through that, and believe me it was very frightening at the time, and if I could help someone and still finish, what more could I do?

My Rocky, my bedrock, my Muse, that place I go to for inspiration, had got me here, helped me dig in and just as important to me, had helped others dig in too and work with them to move on when they felt there was nothing left.

I recalled a talk by Lord Digby Jones, which he gave many years ago now, but that is still relevant. He talked about his life and times, and one story in particular stayed with me and this was when he was at officer school. There were four of them and they had the infamous assault course which was, by all accounts, gruelling, but these were men in their prime and they wanted to beat the course record. They blasted off at the start and three of the four hared across the line eagerly looking to see if they had indeed broken the current record and would be recorded in the annals of time... they were told that they failed. They failed as one was left behind; they failed as they misunderstood what the task was actually about; they failed as they put self-interest first. Lord Digby Jones said that that was a great lesson for him. It was for me too, and instances of how this has resonated will follow in the subsequent chapters.

Ask yourself, are you haring through or are you taking people with you? Are you all about self-interest or is there a bigger prize? Truth be told, I don't know if I saved the guy's life that day, but it did get me thinking about my purpose and if indeed I had it in me to save not only one life, but lives.

EXERCISE TIME: PUSH YOUR BOUNDARIES

Sign up for a challenge that scares you, physical or mental, you decide, just sign up and prepare. Don't think about it too much – just do it. That gap between what you think you can and what you actually can shrinks immediately! And if you are a brave one, who can you take with you on the journey?

THE R.O.C.K.Y ROAD
FOR TEAM HOYT

Rise – Other parents, when given the opportunity to walk away by the medical professionals, may have walked, but not the Hoyt tribe. They decide to run – TOGETHER. Dick wanted his boy to have the same life and opportunities in spite of his cerebral palsy. They not only rise, they lift us all with their story!

Obstacles – The demands of bringing up a family is hard enough and then they willingly take on the challenge of bringing up their quadriplegic son.

Choices – They had a choice, from the outset. They chose life, but they didn't end there. When Rick saw the fun run to raise some money for a good cause – like Goggins in the previous chapter – they found that warrior mode and started running. Because Rick shared with his Dad that when they were out there running he felt like he wasn't disabled, his Dad took this and amplified it. From there they went to marathon running and then IRONMAN® triathlons. They could have stayed at home and perhaps felt sorry for their lot in life, but NO not Team Hoyt – they decided to fly together.

Kaizen – They got faster and Dick says in his 60s that he was faster than when he was at 18 (yes you read that right). When you have a purpose it is truly amazing what can be achieved. Please check this father-son team out on YouTube, it will lift you higher. They have a statue in Boston to celebrate their awesomeness. Let me ask, if you were to have a statue of

You, what would it look like? The Hoyts are running, but what would yours look like? Picture it for a moment, what would you be wearing, what would you be doing that someone should choose to sculpt a statue of you?

You – This chapter is rightly entitled Family as this duo show us what is possible when we have each other's backs and are there for each other. If you hold up the mirror, how is your family dynamic working out for you? Are you the Dick Hoyt figure stepping up to make your child an athlete in spite of life's cards? Are you the Rick figure, dreaming big and finding a way to ascend from life's limitations? Consider YOU as part of your family. If you like the view, well done! If not, take action. It is never too late to be the best Dad, Mum, son, daughter; it is within your hands. Are you taking on life with your family together? As one? Getting across any finishing line feels good – getting others across the line with you is so much sweeter, fulfilling and bigger than any medal you will receive. Family means different things to different folks of course, but be clear about what it means to you, that way you will know if you have been successful. Again this is *your* idea of success.

. . . .

MUSEUM OF MOMENTUM TOUR

Think Team Hoyt when you are doing your thing and taking on the world – take your family with you. It is a balancing act to get everyone on the same bus, not everyone likes the direction of travel, but that same bus is the shelter and forward momentum, let us keep moving forward and taking people with us.

The Hoyts are a breed apart and holding them up as a mirror on family is a little unfair, they stand alone together. They have taken on challenges and life as one.

CHAPTER III:

TIME

WILLIAM SHAKESPEARE

. . . .

"All the world's a stage,
And all the men and women merely players;
They have their exit and their entrances;
And one man in his time plays many parts,
His acts being seven ages... ... ...
Sans teeth, sans eyes, sans taste, sans everything."
(As you like it – Act II Scene VII)

William Shakespeare

Time: What is measured in minutes, hours, days, etc. The time when something happens or when something should happen.

. . . .

Here we attempt to pull back the curtain on time. What is time? Your time? What is inspiration? Your inspiration? If we don't value the days we have then, frankly, it doesn't matter how inspired you are, you are nothing but an empty drum. Time is time, people – it is precious so make much of it. Moreover, this life business cannot be about how much money you have. All this does is give you choices, it doesn't make you happier. You and the people you choose to surround yourself with can make you happier.

We are only trustees. It is true that we are custodians of the present and no more. Of course it would be great if there was a statue of each of us, to be there as a constant reminder of our good deeds etc, but this will not be the case for 99.9 per cent of us. Shakespeare has earned his many statues and busts in Stratford-upon-Avon, with his skill and artistry. It could be said that time has been a cruel mistress to Shakespeare, as other than his prolific writing career little is known about our Shakespeare. His level of creativity has pushed him from backwater playwright to something akin to myth. Even though he is interred in Holy Trinity Church in Stratford-upon-Avon, some say he never existed, or if he did it was the other bloke what did the writing (nod to Morecambe and Wise). The debate rages on, let us agree though that Shakespeare wrote at least

37 plays: 17 comedies, 10 historical, 10 tragedies and more than 150 poems known as Sonnets.

His collected works survive and thrive for us to this day and are a thing of beauty. It's an undeniable truth, inspiring operas, paintings, books, musicals and films – so what is it about this Warwickshire lad that did, does and will inspire until the end of time? The answer is TIME.

Take "Romeo and Juliet" for example. Romeo is in love with another at the start of the play and yet by the end of the play (spoiler alert), he takes his own life for the love of Juliet. Melodramatic your critic barks – wrong. This is a time of plague and think about the longevity of folks back then; you often didn't get "threescore and ten", you were checking out much earlier and if the chances of your untimely end might have been hastened because of a plague, then you will live in the moment as that may be all you've got. Look back just to the Second World War – with the threat of the Blitz where cities could be decimated, your house flattened, streets wiped off the face of the planet, people lived harder as they were in real danger every night. You need to understand that sense of urgency, that "time" to get why they act how they acted.

It is not my role to sell you theatre tickets and convince you that Shakespeare is "The man", we don't need to sell you tickets as you have bought into The R.O.C.K.Y Project and you have your very own ticket to our very own theatre. After all, what does theatre mean? It means "seeing place," this and all chapters use our Ambassadors of Rocky, they are our Players, if you like and at the MUSEum we get to see and hear from them on how they lived, benefit from their lesson/s and make our world richer.

"Romeo & Juliet" is not only a play about love, it is a play to help you be a better parent, to choose life. Everytime we see that play we hope for a different ending, we know how it is going to end, but each time we hope she will wake up that little bit earlier. Alas no, and the play rolls on – it has to end this way; it is through the tragedy that we can learn and not let that be our story, whether lover, parent or friend. Have you noticed that no one ever leaves the theatre before the end? They know what's going to happen but they have to stay, like that moth drawn to the light, so too, we must bear witness. These "star-crossed lovers," are forever doomed, they shared a handful of days together and tragically could only escape by their own hand; indeed, "Never was there a tale of more woe than that of Juliet and her Romeo." I hear you saying, "Hey! This is not called The Romeo Project! Get on with the Rocky stuff!" This is good stuff though, think about it, if you can understand your time, your place and how to live the life you want to lead when the world is telling you "No", you are living on purpose. Let's look at a few who are doing just that, defying convention, living THE life, THEIR life:

. . . .

GENERATION ROCKY – (AGE IS JUST A NUMBER AFTER YOUR NAME)

Take a look around at what is going on and has been going on for sometime now, quietly through the last couple of decades. We are evolving at a rate not seen since we came into being. Making choices that previous generations wouldn't have given themselves permission to take on bucking what society expects of them.

CYCLING AT 105-YEARS-OLD?

4th January 2007: 105-year-old Frenchman Robert Marchand sets a new one-hour cycling record for his age – 14.01 miles in the national velodrome in Saint-Quentin-en-Yvelines west of Paris to the cheers of hundreds of spectators – and when he had finished he said he could have gone faster.

SKYDIVING AT 103-YEARS-OLD?

3rd July 2020: Alfred Blaschke became The Guiness World Record Holder for the oldest tandem parachute jump. We are living longer, but that is not enough – it is how we fill this time.

People have won Olympic Gold medals in their 60s. What about our very own Captain Tom "Tomorrow will be a good day" Moore? In 2020 aged 99-years-old, he decided to walk 100 laps of his garden before his 100th birthday to help raise £1,000 for the NHS. He did it and more, raising over £32 million.

Only 20 years ago we were surviving to around age 70 and then shuffling off – not a bit of it with these fine fellows! And

Warren Buffett, 91 years young, CEO of Berkshire Hathaway Inc. and one of the wealthiest men on the planet.

Richard Branson, head of Virgin Group Limited, was 70-years-old when he became an 'astronaut' as his company Virgin Galactic got him and his crew into space – 70-years-old! Can you see how the world is changing, how we are changing, our expectations of ourselves are literally getting higher and higher and that's okay, because we'll do them anyway.

AND WHAT ABOUT TOM BRADY?

Age 44 and playing in the NFL as one of the most successful quarterbacks of all time for the last 21 years, winning most valued player (MVP) year after year. They say he is relentless, they say it is his work ethic, they say it is because he has grit. To be at the top of his game after all these years, he must be doing something different, or something has awoken in him to not quit, to keep going when many would have retired – but not a bit of it for this guy in an industry where athletes have an average career span of five years, an average age of 28-years-old and most retire in their mid to late 30s, but Brady marches on! He is definitely part of the Rocky Generation, and if he is doing it then all those hundreds of thousands that watch him must be asking themselves questions about what they could be doing at age 44 and beyond (the way he is going).

Is there a superhuman gene (within us all) awakening, some mutation happening within us? Steven Kotler argues, "It's always been about us – all of us – doing impossible deeds. It is our future that is on the line. We can harness flow and ride the wave of possibility that is abundance or we can get dashed upon the rocks of half-hearted measures."[7] (The Rise of Superman, Steven Kotler).

EXERCISE TIME: WHAT LIFE DO YOU WANT TO LIVE?

Look at your hands, the skin, your fingers, your face and hair, see you as you are. Now let us use our imaginations. In your mind's eye picture your ten-year-old self walking towards you, slowly coming into focus. Look at their hands, skin, hair, clothes, see how time has defined them – if they could tell you one thing of the life you are yet to have, what would it be? Fast forward now to the older you at 70 years, walking towards you, the way you look at this moment, and see how time has sculpted you, what would that person say? What do you want that person to say to you?

"We had a wonderful life – well done!"

"We made our mark."

---

[7] Steven Kotler, (2014), *The Rise of Superman: Decoding the Science of Ultimate Human Performance*, Houghton Mifflin Harcourt

"You did the best with what you had."

What you do not want to hear is:

"Why did you let our dreams die?"

"Why did you settle?"

"The world is big but you hardly scratched the surface."

Doing this exercise with the likes of the younger Churchill or Ali, for example, their younger selves had no idea of the impact they would have. Even though Ali hailed himself as "The Greatest," he was to achieve so much more through his actions regarding the Vietnam War and civil rights – being world champion merely provided him a platform to send ripples around the world. Churchill too, born into nobility and becoming the voice of resistance to a world threat, where his older self resonated throughout the known world as he took a defiant stand. Their reverberations will go on and on. Anyone who saw Ali light the Olympic torch in Atlanta 1996 must have been moved or you are dead already. For people like these, who did indeed, *seize* their day, what would they say to their younger selves, what whispers? We can only imagine. This is a theme we will revisit; it is a theme you should revisit.

Do this exercise: think about all you have done to this point, all you want to do and let your older self mentor you and get the life you want (the life that your older self has already lived) mapped, and live it.

PRINCE HAL THE UNDERDOG BECOMES KING HENRY V AND THE AGINCOURT HERO

One of Shakespeare's underdogs is Prince Hal who, in Henry IV parts I & II, is a Prince who runs about with the Old Rascal Knight Sir John Falstaff, forsaking his role and position. However, towards the end of the play he answers the call and his shining moment is on the Battlefield of Agincourt. His army had endured and won the Battle of Harfleur three weeks earlier, again against the odds, but with Henry's conviction, will and determination, as penned by Shakespeare in Henry V, "Once more unto the breach dear friends, once more." The English army of some 6,000 then faced a great French force of around 20,000, outnumbered at least three to one. The English force had marched for 200 miles and were spent. Yet the King found his voice on that fateful day, St Crispin's day, 25th October 1415, to rally the troops, win the battle, which would be pivotal in bringing the 100 years war to it's conclusion.

Henry V:
This day is called the feast of Crispian:
He that outlives this day, and comes safe home,
Will stand a tip-toe when the day is named,
And rouse him at the name of Crispian.
He that shall live this day, and see old age,
Will yearly on the vigil feast his neighbours,
And say 'To-morrow is Saint Crispian.'
Then will he strip his sleeve and show his scars.
And say 'These wounds I had on Crispin's day.'
Old men forget: yet all shall be forgot,
But he'll remember with advantages
What feats he did that day.
Henry V, Act IV, Scene III

Rousing, eh? Do you see how Shakespeare uses time? It is years hence from this moment, but you will remember your greatness, your achievements, so dare greatly, chalk them up. I say to YOU – "Once more unto the breach!", I say to YOU, "Old men forget, yet all shall be forgot, but YOU'LL remember with advantages, what feats YOU did that day!" So what is "that day" to you? What does it look like? Consider it, shape it, is it that promotion, that new business, that challenge you have set yourself? You decide.

ROCKY FILENAME

SHAKESPEARE
William Shakespeare

OCCUPATION	Poet, Actor & Playwright
MADE THEIR ENTRANCE	23rd April 1564 Stratford-upon-Avon, England
TOOK THEIR LAST BOW	23rd April 1616 Stratford-upon-Avon, England
EDUCATION	King's New School (now King Edward VI Grammar School) Stratford-upon-Avon, England
ORIGINALLY	Son of a Glover
AKA	The Greatest Playwright that ever lived
ACHIEVEMENTS (SOME OF..)	General consensus is that he wrote 37 plays Wordage (tome = plays and Sonnets): 880,000+ Created 1700 new words

"Alas, poor Yorick! I knew him, Horatio: a fellow of infinite jest, of most excellent fancy: he hath borne me on his back a thousand times; and now, how abhorred in my imagination it is! My gorge rises at it. Here hung those lips that I have kiss'd I know not how oft. Where be your gibes now? your gambols? your songs? your flashes of merriment, that were wont to set the table on a roar? Not one now, to mock your own grinning?"
Hamlet, Act V, Scene I

Like it or not, one day you will look like Yorick, so will your friends, family and clients. Shakespeare knew all too well about the fragility of life and Hamlet's tender moment with the family's long-lost clown puts us in touch with our own mortality. If you know this is our destination, surely you should do something about it – we should dance like a dervish, we should celebrate life, this is part of our time here. For those out there who are selling a product year in year out, I am not speaking to you, but to those who engage and wish to engage on a higher level I say to you: life is not a rehearsal. We all know there is a final bow coming, so before then let us do great things, let us surprise ourselves and the ones around us. Inspire and be inspired. In our lives there are challenges, bad stuff happens, but good stuff happens too and the challenge is to be the perpetrators of more good and make much of our time here?

I mentioned the Stoics in Chapter 1 and visiting some of the WWI Memorials in Northern France really brought it home – that these lost boys, men and women would give *anything* for another day, that became a memento mori for me. Normally a memento mori is an object that folk would carry around hundreds of years ago as a constant reminder. For me, however, my memento mori is that place, Theipval, where everything those young men could do, or be, was taken away from them.

Memento Mori: An object serving as a warning or reminder of death/the Latin phrase means literally, 'remember (that you have) to die'.

. . . .

If all this Latin and olde English is too much, here is the message in pop speak:

> *"Soon I'll be 60 years old, will I make the world as cold or will I have a lot of children who can hold me? Soon I'll be 60 years old..." 7 Years (Lukas Graham)*[8]

He gets that passing of time – in a blink, you are 60! Dear reader, if you haven't got the message already, if it hasn't broken through, please make much of time BEFORE YOU ARE 60. Or if you are 60, make much of time before you are 80. And if you're 80... You get the picture.

How the times they are a changin'. Here is a New York Times article from 1st November 1976. It highlights how Rocky's rise was impossible, but happened nevertheless. Here's our very own Rocky time machine, buckle up, next stop November '76:

. . . .

[8] Lukas Graham, *7 Years*, Lukas Graham (Blue Album), released 2015, Copenhagen Records

'ROCKY ISN'T BASED ON ME,' SAYS STALLONE, 'BUT WE BOTH WENT THE DISTANCE'[9]

"A year ago, Sylvester Stallone had $106 in the bank. His wife was pregnant, his bull mastiff was starving and he couldn't pay the rent on his seedy Hollywood apartment. What to do? Well, one answer was that Stallone, a sometime actor-turned-screenwriter, could sit down and in 3 and a half days write a screenplay with a meaty starring role in it for himself, persuade someone to film it, and wind up a millionaire. Improbable? ''You know,'' he said, returning to the subject of ''Rocky,'' ''If nothing else comes out of that film in the way of awards and accolades, it will still show that an unknown quantity, a totally unmarketable person, can produce a diamond in the rough, a gem. And there are a lot more people like me out there too, people whose chosen profession denies them opportunity.''

Rocky racing up the stairs to "Gonna fly now" or the elderly Rocky in Creed still fighting (cancer), slowly, ever so slowly, managing the stairs, one step at a time. This is no less of an achievement. While we have our health, we are abundantly rich. Health is wealth! While we can run up the stairs, let us run up the stairs, because the time will soon come when we will look up at them and smile and think, "Back in the day I used to be able to run up these." Time can be a cruel mistress but a lot of this is in our minds. We just get comfortable, we

[9] Judy Klemesrud, (1976), ''Rocky Isn't Based on Me,' Says Stallone, 'But We Both Went the Distance'', New York Times, 28 November

stop pushing, we settle. What can you do to help you? Diet, improve your CV, decide what bad habits you would like to replace for good ones? Right now.

Just as Stallone created his alter ego, his nom de guerre, I did too. I was inspired by the Rocky films as far back as a child. It would be many, many years later, that my childhood inspiration would lead to a renaissance, just as Michelangelo, Shakespeare and Da Vinci as renaissance men were inspired by the Greeks and Romans before them.

Renaissance: the period in Europe during the 14th, 15th, and 16th centuries when people became interested in the ideas and culture of ancient Greece and Rome and used these influences in their own art, literature, etc.

. . . .

A renewal of life, vigor, interest, rebirth, revival.

. . . .

The renaissance is one of the most fascinating periods in human history. Why was it such a portentous moment in our evolution? Shakespeare and Michelangelo lend their creative mastery to define an age and as torch bearers of their time perhaps it was simply that they realised that TIME was the currency. Shakespeare wrote mostly in verse following iambic pentameter (a ten-syllable pattern along rhyming scheme). It is almost a morse code passed down through the ages; an enduring message:

> "Like as the waves make towards the pebbl'd shore,
> So do our minutes hasten to their end;
> Each changing place with that which goes before,
> In sequent toil all forwards do contend."
> Sonnet 60, William Shakespeare

Other than perhaps the digital evolutions that we are currently going through, not since the renaissance have so many people become so inspired and as such, changed the world around them. Indeed they created a legacy that has lasted hundreds of years after their deaths. They did not take their artistry to the grave, they did not die and take their sonnets and humanity back to the soil. They celebrated time, they celebrated that we need to do all we can do, be all we can be, say all we can say before our time is up. I am not saying live a hedonistic life, not at all, I am saying we must all strive to have a meaningful life. The sentiment of Carpe Diem to me means make the best life you can for yourself today. The future will always be that place in the future that you will never quite get to, live in the present but make that future place and that future self the best it can be. Like Michelangelo's David, don't stop once you have the body, bring it to life, let us see the veins and the definition; don't settle.

Just as then, we are fiercely aware of the passing of time in the digital age. We can get information instantly, we have machines to do jobs which we perceive as too menial for humans, all so that we can focus on our time – albeit many use this time to watch the box set of Breaking Bad or Game of Thrones. Yes I have seen them, and they are compelling; however my point is that we stop doing the physical work to vegetate. We do not have a challenge in our lives so we go to the gym and put ourselves through hell. Rather than painting the house, cleaning the house or even choosing to walk instead of drive, we outsource much that we could do ourselves. The digital age has empowered us but at what expense? If we over indulge, we can have an operation to remove the fatty tissue. There are numerous drugs to help us with this, that and the other, ignoring the natural chemicals that are within us, such as endorphins and serotonin.

. . . .

iROCKY

I should have known that there was something different about my thinking as I wanted to start reading Shakespeare in my first year of secondary school (I didn't know who he was but people seemed to revere him even at that time, so I thought that there must be something to him). There was only one of his great tomes kicking around on the shelf, it was Henry IV Part I. Ironically, 11 years later, it was a speech from that same play that got me my place at Guildhall (GSMD).

By having that sense of Memento mori, we have to be grateful for the time we have and make it count. Here's an idea: how about doing more, or if you are new to this, try some random acts of kindness (RAOK). This means, rather than dropping a coin at the feet of that homeless man, which is the easy way out, why not get him a hot drink, some food, or even talk to him. Why can't we be the ones to offer the hand, the shoulder in times of need, be the good shepherd, samaritan, good soul? How about, instead of ploughing your way through all the Rocky films, or the Breaking Bad box set or Game of Thrones multi-series, you volunteer for an hour in the local soup kitchen, or at a local hospice. Make your life count more and help make others' lives count just as much too – I dare you!

DECEMBER 31ST

Think for a moment about New Year's Eve, it's a time when we can be surrounded by our friends and family, celebrating the arrival of the New Year, yet we always get a sense of melancholy, don't we, as we say goodbye to the current year and think about absent friends and those that we lost along the way. This night of all nights is really what it's all about:

◊ Gratitude – celebrating the people you have in your life right now, we even call those dear ones who aren't in the room to shout "HAPPY NEW YEAR!", it's important to acknowledge that we have had a year together and God willing we have this one too!

◇ Remembrance – raising a glass for those who have left the dance floor; perhaps tears come, perhaps you smile as you celebrate their memory.

Then what do we do? We dance on. If you are truly grateful for not only your time, but what you have done with your time, you party, you dance on.

I don't know how you see in the New Year – for the Bibb's we head North to Scotland for Hogmanay. Hogmanay is the Scottish way to ring out the old and bring in the new. We surround ourselves with family, have some old-fashioned games and catching up, and then we dress in our finest, and ceilidh (like it's 1999!). There's a piper, a ceilidh and dancing, and it is okay if you don't know the moves, just bring your best highland fling, your best "omcha, omcha, omcha!", shoulders going, feet a-shuffling, much dancing, much singing, much family time – acknowledging the year past and if we had made much of time and carry the hope through to the New Year, then that sense of celebration will continue to the dawn and beyond! Why do I mention 31 December? Because it is an obvious marker of everyone's time – that time of reflection: you and everyone else in the room was given 8,760 hours for that year – did you make much of that time? Moving forward, what are you going to do with the next allocation of 8,760 hours? Sleepwalk through them? Stay on auto pilot? Never leave your comfort zone? Or are you going to do something to improve your happiness, your legacy, your destiny even, so that for this next coming last day of December you will revel in all that you have achieved and can't wait for the clock to reset? So you can just get better and have more laughter at year's end, fewer tears, less regret, more accomplishment and you are looking toward the horizon and keen for the dawn to start at January 1, so you can get after it.

YOUR MISSION HOGMANAY – SHOULD YOU CHOOSE TO ACCEPT IT...

You might be picking this book up in the summer or it might have been a Christmas present; either way, you can make a promise to yourself to do all that you can now, so that when your next December 31st comes, you will be at least one percent happier than last New Year's Eve. If possible make sure you are with your nearest and dearest and for those who aren't in the room – let them know how much they mean to you (Hey Critic Brain – just try it, don't judge it and see what happens). Time people, it is all about time, what you do with it and who you spend it with, don't just let it slide.

Shakespeare marked time in his verse, counted the beats, like a pulse beating through until Act V. None of us know when our Act V will be, but let me tell you when the doctor says you have a year to live, you feel that beat, those relationships get stronger and your will to live, to enjoy every moment – to Carpe

Diem becomes the strongest it has ever been. The lesson: DON'T WAIT FOR THAT DAY – seize it now.

Shakespeare's Hamlet is not a great advocate for living this way, to Carpe Diem, to seize the day; he prevaricates all through the play, feigning madness and putting on a play "The MouseTrap" and keeps us in suspense until Act V, even after the visitations from his late father, telling him that he was killed by his own brother and Hamlet must avenge him. He thinks about his soul and what murder means, some of the biggies, but it is only after his Mum has been poisoned that he springs into action and kills his Uncle who, did indeed kill Hamlet's father and then married his own brother's wife. Now, I am sure that none of my readers will be having such a dilemma as being haunted by a parent to kill their Uncle who has married their own sister-in-law – this I am sure was a unique Danish problem for back in the day BUT, we all get a touch of "The Hamlets": talking, rather than doing, around the big challenges of our life TODAY – relationships, business, freedoms, time.

I am not suggesting for a moment that you set about to kill anyone – let me get that disclaimer out there – what you do need to kill is the time thief "procrastination." If you have something you want to do THIS YEAR, you have 8,760 hours to get it done, no more, no less. If you just talk about it for an hour guess what? 8,759 left to go and so the sand falls through the hourglass, and you are no nearer there. So what can we do about this? The simple thing is to give it a date: "Done by." Whatever you want to do this year, just put a date next to it and do it by then. Too Simple? No, it is not. We often get in our own way, so just put a date on it. Yes, there will be obstacles but you have given yourself time to recognise them and overcome them.

My mentor asked me very early doors, "What is the difference between a dream and a goal?" The answer was/is a goal has a date next to it and a dream doesn't. Now I am sorry if your world has just been rocked because you like pushing that "dream" that you have back to next year and next year, "I am writing a book," "I am going to learn to play guitar," "I'm going to start a business...." Give it a date and it will happen or by committing it to a time, if you pass it and have not achieved it, you will realise you probably didn't want it bad enough in the first place. If you do commit though and even get to just 80 per cent then you are living the dream and this is what The R.O.C.K.Y Project is all about; not leaving stuff on the shelf, but living with intention and striving to be all that you can be and helping others along the way.

Here's another one, which might make some of the hairs on the back of your arm stand up. As you know, I am a writer and one of the days when writing this book I had a moment... My young daughter and friends wanted to go and see a concert. I said okay, but only if I accompanied them into Birmingham and took them to the door, and was there when the concert finished. We travelled into the city, I duly fulfilled my first pledge to get them to the concert. I told them that, if there were any problems, I would be in the lobby of The Radisson Blu, beavering away on my book. The lobby-come-bar area was not as quiet as I hoped it would be. It was race week at Cheltenham and some punters had camped there for the week. There I was, Macbook, iPad, pad and pen sprawled in front of me – to all the world I was working, indisposed and on a mission. To all the world that is except one man, who came up to me, two drinks in hand and started talking to me, oblivious that I was in author mode and that I was penning a best seller.

He told me his life story (can't blame him, as this happens to me ALL the time), how he met his wife at uni, he a successful businessman and she a doctor, that they had had a child recently, but then the picture changed. He lost it all, his wife had thrown him out, he was an alcoholic, had been to all the groups, tried everything, they had the baby and this was his last chance to shape up, but the drink had got him bad. I listened to him and he was keen to show me his favourite football team, the best time he called it, so I handed over my iPad and he showed me Manchester United winning, the goals, the Treble. His phone was pinging with message alerts, he responded. There were missed calls, he ignored them. He told me about a friend of his who was texting him, trying to take his life and now they use each other as back up. He sent him a text back. An hour or two went by and he wanted to buy me a drink. I said I would buy him a coffee and he agreed. I left him with my iPad and went to the bar. I eventually got served, but when I turned from the bar with the coffees, he was gone. I finished up with the chapter that I had started, drank my coffee and started to pack up as I had a gaggle of teenagers I had promised to meet post concert.

I made to leave but the man returned, coming straight over to me and saying he would like to introduce me to his wife, "But I thought you said she had kicked you out?" I asked. He explained she had tracked him down. I followed him. We reached the door, he knocked and a woman answered. Behind her on the double bed I saw the young child/infant. She self consciously put her hair behind her ear and said, "Well this is awkward," and indeed it was. I was a perfect stranger. She invited me in, her husband, my bar buddy, following behind. I said, "This must be your daughter," and we made small talk. Then there was another knock on the door. She answered it, and I saw it was the police, "Yes this is my husband," she said, and the police asked if they could have a word with him, taking him into another room (goosebump moment).

When the door closed she came over to me and said, "Thank you for being with my husband tonight," I replied something like, "Not at all/No worries," and then she held my hand and said, "No, thank you for being here. My husband came here to kill himself, but you listened to him," she squeezed my hand, "You are an Angel." What can you say when someone says something like that to you? Moreover, when you have spent time with someone and you hear their intentions were to depart this world, to give up that oh so precious gift that is life, you go numb. We didn't swap numbers, I must have just mumbled something and said I had to go and collect the girls who'd be waiting for me. I found the lift, headed down and, zombie-like, left the lobby. The girls were waiting for me as the concert had ended and they were worried about me. There was a police car parked up in front of the hotel. When the girls asked why I wasn't there I pointed to the police car and told them the tale. Apologising for not being there, they of course understood.

What is the point of sharing this dramatic true story with you? Well I gave him TIME, that was all, and continuing this theme of the Hero's Journey, part of which was me taking up the IRONMAN® event journey which in turn led me to start writing about it and there I was late one night in Birmingham, a man was in pain and I gave him an ear and then got called an angel. Where does your time go? Are there those in your life, in your circle, in your tribe, who could do with your ears? You can never tell just by looking at someone if they are happy.

Shakespeare is perhaps the best 'Time' advocate: the English language from 500 years ago is not everyone's cup of tea, but there is truth and beauty in there. Time is a constant in all our lives and it is a constant theme in his works, "And nothing 'gainst Time's scythe can make defence" (Sonnet 12). Let us all make much of time, don't waste it. This chapter went into dark cave mode – we talked about death and loss, but it is only through appreciating that one day we will be history rather than present, by looking at the ones we have lost in our lives and knowing that one day we too will be lost to time, that we feel alive.

We have to feel our pulse rather than it being an unrespected background hum. Only by knowing that one day we shall pass, and appreciating and respecting that fact, can we truly live today with a greater sense of Carpe Diem, with a greater sense of gratitude, and with more sense to our lives and the lives of others. As the sand continues to fall through your hourglass do not get buried by the accumulating grains. Let us pull ourselves up and stand on top of the sand dune that is our life and take action.

EXERCISE TIME: WRITE A LETTER TO YOURSELF

Write a letter to yourself. If you're brave enough, write two!

Step 1: The first letter is from your older self, ten years ago. What would you have written to yourself, what was that audacious goal you were hankering after? What were your challenges, obstacles? What did your world look like then? Time travel back to that place – like Stallone in that rundown apartment – rock bottom but dreaming of Rocky to escape, but not just dreaming, writing and writing to make it happen. Even when he did get interest, he stuck to his guns – he thought, he said, he lived, "No I am Rocky, this is my story." So what is your story and if you had to channel it over the past ten years what does that journey look like? Perhaps not as rags to riches as Stallone, perhaps you have had a much larger exponential curve – chart it, not for me but for you. *IMPORTANT* once you have written it, reread it and note how you feel.

Step 2: Now write a future letter to yourself. You are HERE but your dream/goal over the next ten years is to be OVER THERE. Be clear about where you are, home, family, business and all the little landmarks along the way and even though this is not a sports book (you could have fooled me, with all this IRONMAN® race stuff, I hear you say, and what about all these sporting icons? I hear you, but the IRONMAN® event was just a vehicle and we all have sporting heroes because they, (a) want to win, be the best and (b) they strive. Please add in your fitness regime. It's no good planning for this great future life if your heart blows up!

If a blank page feels a little intimidating and you're not sure where to start, reach out to me for a bit of that Rocky magic. As you're learning, every hero needs a mentor and I'm here to be yours if you need that extra push. You can reach me at **therockyprojectexperience@gmail.com**

Whether you like poetry or not, here was a man, Shakespeare, whose works live on and for the purposes of this book their magic does too. What say you? Which of your words will echo through time? What are your words doing now and if your Completed Works were assembled what would that look like? Would the overarching theme be that you did much with your time?

. . . .

THE R.O.C.K.Y ROAD FOR WILLIAM SHAKESPEARE

Rise – In spite of his background and education, Shakespeare took up the quill and held his own with his contemporaries. More than this, his sense of truth, craft and beauty shone through. We still go to see his "Romeo & Juliet" and hope that the ending will be different this time. We are involved with these star-crossed lovers, Hamlet keeps us asking, "To be or not to be, that is the question..." We are still discussing it and perhaps will, until the end of days. We revel in Nick Bottom, his transformation and the mechanicals, and are transported to that magical world of Midsummer Nights Dream.

Obstacles – The loss of a child is devastating. Shakespeare used the loss of his son Hamnet, the only way he knew how and that was to write, to heal through creation. His family were in Stratford-upon-Avon, but London was the place to be seen and get the success for his work.

Choices – He could have settled for parochial life, he could have been swept away with the tsunami of grief in losing a child. He chose his work and that has stood the test of time, and is a testament to his world view based on his life experiences, good and bad.

Kaizen – Look at the tomes of his work; by the time he gets to the *Tempest* he is ready to "Drown my books." From the early plays to his last, there is truth and something overlooked about our Shakespeare is that he was not limited by language – he was happy to make up a new word to fit with the truth, and the Iambic pentameter. Not constrained by words that existed, he invented new ones. He invented words – surely he was bigger than his time.

You – If this is your time what are you doing about it? Are you using that creative mind to express yourself, your business, your life? Remember we cannot invent more time, we can only make much of the time we have. Ask yourself now, are you?

. . . .

MUSEUM OF MOMENTUM TOUR

So my Projectarians, take a moment and consider stepping into that horseshoe table surrounded by our Hall of Famers, your board members, and there's Shakespeare giving you this wake up call. Time passes, listen... There it goes, whether you are watching box sets of Downton Abbey (running time of one day, 23.5 hours), Breaking Bad (running time two days, 14 hours), Game of Thrones (running time two days, 22 hours and 14 minutes), meditating on the wonders of the world or sleeping it away, time passes.

Shakespeare holds up a clock to us. If you listen closely he is telling you to make it count, make it count, make it count. When your time is up, whether you are a CEO, COO, Chairman or President, your journey is at an end. So use it, respect it and don't waste it.

CHAPTER IV:
COACH

MUHAMMAD ALI

. . . .

"I know where I'm going and I know the truth, and I don't have to be what you want me to be. I'm free to be what I want."[10]

Muhammad Ali

---

[10] Robert Lipsyte, (1964), 'Clay Discusses his Future, Liston and Black Muslims', *New York Times*, 27 February, available at: archive.nytimes.com/www.nytimes.com/books/98/10/25/specials/ali-future.html

Coach: a person who trains a person or team in sport.

....

A good coach, like a good teacher, awakens something in us. They remind us that we can do something and they make us believe. If you don't believe me, what about Galileo? He knew a thing or two, the philosopher, astronomer and mathematician said, "We can't teach people anything. We can only help them to discover it within themselves," (Galileo Galilei). This is true and whilst we are discovering what we have within ourselves, we will bring in that little known philosopher Rocky, who, whilst not as lyrical as Shakespeare or as deep as Galileo, has a training style that goes straight to the heart: "What's can't? There ain't no can'ts, there's no can'ts" (Mickey from Rocky II).

So to our real-life champion of the ring. Ali was more than just a boxer though. In this chapter we take the complete man, not just the boxer that everyone knows, and let his wisdom coach us. We let his actions show us and we let his words discover something within ourselves. Ali was 54 years old when he stood in Atlanta holding the Olympic torch to open the 1996 Olympic Games. Here he stood and the world was holding its breath. The Champ looked weak, vulnerable and the effects of Parkinson's were clearly visible, and taking their toll on him. Yet there he stood, for the world to see. To me, he stood as if to say "Undefeated," defiantly fighting his illness with the world watching. Ali held the torch aloft and we watched. This wasn't the first time for him – he had been doing it all his life and now he is holding the torch to relight your fire, to relight your life.

INTRODUCING MUHAMMAD ALI

It all began for Ali (then Cassius Marcellus Clay Jnr.) when he had his bicycle stolen. He reported it to a police officer and, as fate would have it, that very same police officer was a part-time trainer for young boxers and he encouraged the young Cassius, then 12 years old, to come and box. He noticed the natural talents of the boy, the boy indeed who would be King!

Speaking of King, it's uncanny, don't you think, that they both (Ali and Billie Jean King) fell into their sport at the same early age. Ali became The World's best in 1964 aged 22 and Billie Jean King in 1966 aged 26.

On Ali: "The kid was electric," Angelo Dundee

Ali had his Dundee, Angelo Dundee. I declare that if Ali needed a coach, then ALL of us need a coach!

ROCKY FILENAME

MUHAMMAD ALI
Muhammad Ali

OCCUPATION	Boxer
MADE THEIR ENTRANCE	17th January 1942, Louisville, Kentucky
TOOK THEIR LAST BOW	3rd June 2016, Scottsdale, Arizona
EDUCATION	Central High School
ORIGINALLY	Born Cassius Marcellus Clay Jnr.
AKA	The Louisville Lip The Greatest Heavyweight Champion of the World
ACHIEVEMENTS	Olympic Gold Medal – Rome 1960 (aged 18) The first three-time Heavyweight Champion of the world Conscientious Objector (Vietnam War) – "I ain't got no quarrel with them Viet Cong." 1999 Sports Illustrated – Sportsperson of the century 1964 His shot at the Heavyweight title and beats Sonny Liston He goes on to defend his title, but his title is stripped from him in 1967 due to him refusing to be drafted to Vietnam – what a man! 1970 Gets back into the ring 1974 "The Rumble in the Jungle" – in Zaire, fights George Foreman and wins the title back (Age 32)

ACHIEVEMENTS CONTINUED	1975 "The Thrilla in Manilla" – in the Philippines, fights Joe Frazier and wins 1978 Beats Leon Spinks to win back the Heavyweight title (Age 36 – the first boxer to achieve this feat and worth also noting that Ali was 10 years older than Spinks). He then retires but makes an ill-advised comeback to two bitter defeats, finally hangs his gloves up 1981, but to me he then holds something much bigger – the torch. Ali becomes THE torchbearer.

THE PASSING OF ALI: 3RD JUNE 2016

It was a sad day when I heard of Ali's passing. I was in the US and the news was everywhere. It was as if someone had turned out a light, the world seemed a little darker without him in it. Others will rise, no doubt, but perhaps not with the amount of charisma, dynamism and skill as Ali. "I am the Greatest!" He was the master of the self fulfilling prophecy!

What can Ali teach us? He is not renowned as a coach, he was too busy creating his legacy as one of the greatest, if not the greatest heavyweight champion of the world, *but* here are some whispers from Ali to you, to coach, to awake, to ignite. Here he stands as our cornerman as we venture through our journey, through our struggles.

Over to you Ali:

ON JOURNEY

"Each time I thought I had achieved my 'life's purpose,' I discovered it was only another step in my journey."[11]

"It isn't the mountains ahead to climb that wear you out; it's the pebble in your shoe."[12]

ON FAMILY

"When it comes to love, compassion, and other feelings of the heart, I am rich."[13]

"At home I am a nice guy: but I don't want the world to know. Humble people, I've found, don't get very far."

"Service to others is the rent you pay for your room here on Earth."

ON TIME

"He who is not courageous enough to take risks will accomplish nothing in life."[14]

[11] Hana Yasmeen Ali and Muhammad Ali, (2005), 'The Soul Of A Butterfly: Reflections on life's journey', *Bantam*

[12] Score Your Goal, (2019), 'Notebook Motivational Journal with Quote by Muhammad Ali', (Motivate Yourself)

[13] Hana Yasmeen Ali and Muhammad Ali, (2005), 'The Soul Of A Butterfly: Reflections on life's journey', *Bantam*

[14] Bernie Linicome, (1977), 'Ali, Louis: The Spectre of Greatness Past', *Fort Lauderdale News*, 14 April

"A man who views the world the same at 50 as he did at 20 has wasted 30 years of his life."[15]

ON COACH

"The fight is won or lost far away from the witnesses, behind the lines, in the gym and out there on the road, long before I dance under those lights."
"I've made my share of mistakes along the way, but if I have changed even one life for the better, I haven't lived in vain."[16]

ON BUSINESS

"Champions are made from something they have deep inside them – a desire, a dream, a vision. They have to have the skill, and the will. But the will must be stronger than the skill."[17]
"I calculate that I took 20,000 punches, but I earned millions and kept a lot of it. I may talk slow, but my mind is OK."

ON CHALLENGE

"Impossible is just a big word thrown around by small men who find it easier to live in the world they've been given than to explore the power they have to change it. Impossible is not a fact. It's an

[15] Barney Martlew, (2015), *Lessons After The Bell: A man who views the world the same at 50 as he did at 20 has wasted 30 years of his life*, WestBowPress
[16] Hana Ali, (2011), 'My dad, Muhammad Ali', *CNN*, 19 June, available at: edition.cnn.com/2011/OPINION/06/19/ali.fathers.day
[17] Muhammad Ali, 10 August 2010

opinion. Impossible is not a declaration. It's a dare. Impossible is potential. Impossible is temporary. Impossible is nothing."[18]

ON MINDSET

"A man who has no imagination has no wings."[19]
"Age is whatever you think it is. You are as old as you think you are."
"I am the greatest. I said that even before I knew I was. I figured that if I said it enough, I would convince the world that I was really the greatest."[20]

ON SUFFERING

"I don't count my sit-ups; I only start counting when it starts hurting because they're the only ones that count."[21]
"Don't quit. Suffer now and live the rest of your life as a champion."

[18] CBS News, (2016), 'Muhammad Ali: In his own words', 5 June, available at: www.cbsnews.com/news/muhammad-ali-in-his-own-words

[19] Jeff Johnson, (2016), 'Muhammad Ali In His Own Words: Six of His Best Quotes to Live By, *NBC News,* 4 June, available at: www.nbcnews.com/news/nbcblk/remembering-muhammad-ali-six-quotes-pack-punch-n585571

[20] Darren Rovell, (2016), 'Muhammad Ali's 10 best quotes', *ESPN,* 3 June, available at: www.espn.co.uk/boxing/story/_/id/15930888/muhammad-ali-10-best-quotes

[21] Darren Rovell, (2016), 'Muhammad Ali's 10 best quotes', *ESPN,* 3 June, available at: www.espn.co.uk/boxing/story/_/id/15930888/muhammad-ali-10-best-quotes

ON ACHIEVEMENT

"The greatest victory in life is to rise above the material things that we once valued most."

"I know where I'm going and I know the truth, and I don't have to be what you want me to be. I'm free to be what I want."[22]

ON INSPIRATION

"I wanted to use my fame and this face that everyone knows so well to help uplift and inspire people around the world."[23]

"I am an ordinary man who worked hard to develop the talent I was given. I believed in myself, and I believe in the goodness of others."

ON LEGACY

"I would like to be remembered as a man who won the heavyweight title three times. Who was humorous and who treated everyone right. As a man who never looked down on those who looked up to him, and who helped as many people as he could. As a man who stood up for his beliefs no matter what. As a man who tried to unite all humankind through faith and love. And if all that's too much, then I guess I'd settle for being remembered only as a great boxer who became

[22] Robert Lipsyte, (1964), 'Clay Discusses his Future, Liston and Black Muslims', *New York Times*, 27 February, available at: archive.nytimes.com/www.nytimes.com/books/98/10/25/specials/ali-future.html

[23] Hana Ali, (2011), 'My dad, Muhammad Ali', *CNN*, 19 June, available at: edition.cnn.com/2011/OPINION/06/19/ali.fathers.day

*a leader and a champion of his people. And I wouldn't
even mind if folks forgot how pretty I was."*[24]

ON ALCHEMY

*"If they can make penicillin out of moldy bread,
you can sure make something out of you."*
*"It's the repetition of affirmations that leads to belief.
And once that belief becomes a deep conviction,
things begin to happen."*[25]

If nothing has jumped out at you here and got inside then reread those quotes! This is a man who not only got to the top of his game, he transcended it. Ali was not just a boxer, this book is not about boxing – it is about your fire, let it burn. Ali's words and actions will fan the flames, listen to him, take counsel and make it count!

. . . .

iROCKY

You cannot be all things to all people, so who is in your corner? In your profession, who is it that coaches you? Inspires you?

[24] Hana Yasmeen Ali and Muhammad Ali, (2005), 'The Soul Of A Butterfly: Reflections on life's journey', *Bantam*

[25] Jeff Johnson, (2016), 'Muhammad Ali In His Own Words: Six of His Best Quotes to Live By, *NBC News*, 4 June, available at: www.nbcnews.com/news/nbcblk/remembering-muhammad-ali-six-quotes-pack-punch-n585571

Come on, even the mighty Usain Bolt has a coach – what makes you so special? Who motivates the motivator? Who picks you up when you are low and celebrates the highs with you? Perhaps a better question for you is, whose corner are you in?

At this point, I'm bringing in one of my friends, who was only a small, diminutive lass, but probably the best fighter I have seen. Her name was Sharon Jones. As fate would have it our mums were maternity ward neighbours in June 1970. We were born in the same hospital, with only a handful of days separating our births'. Years passed, the wheel turned and doing my A-levels meant having to travel to different schools. Sharon came up to me after the first week and asked if my mum is called Penny, I said yes and then she told the story of how our mums met. We became friends, did our studies and then went on with our separate lives.

Whilst at drama school in London, I got a call telling me she had cancer, was not in great shape, and was in hospital. She was 24 years old. Ironically, she was in the same hospital where our mums met and where we both greeted this world. She had been given a whole load of cancer treatment to try and stop the virulent strain, but it was not working.

I jumped on a train to see her, and on my arrival (I was told later that she put a wig on for my benefit) what a girl I found! She was going through hell but she wore a wig to help *me* feel okay. Sharon the fighter came through this, perhaps through her will power alone. 'Courageously' is a word that tends to get thrown around but she typified courageously.

When the doctors said that they were only left with the option to use trial/experimental drugs, as a last chance, she bravely agreed and she beat it. She beat it. She went back to work at The Council House in Birmingham and continued with her great work in the county's fostering programme. When she recovered from her first bout of cancer treatment, she decided to hold a fundraiser at the Grand Council House in Birmingham to raise money for the hospital that cared for her – a wonderful gesture.

She could have sat back and felt sorry for herself, but not a bit of it. She could have curled up and given up – no way. What I can still hear her say, after all this time is: "Do it, do it." Who do you have in your life who is in your corner willing you on, and cheering you on? Or are you that cornerman/woman, a fixed point, focused and willing on your son/daughter/friend/spouse/relative? Sharon knew that a dream of mine was to act with the Royal Shakespeare Company. Even with all she had going on, she found an ad for a play that they were doing called "Thyestes" and encouraged me to audition. I did, got the part and achieved that dream because of her.

Despite beating cancer, her fight continued. The drugs seriously affected her immune system resulting in her requiring a lung transplant. In 2003 a donor was found, but the operation was sadly unsuccessful and we lost her, she was 33. However, it was important to her to get her affairs in order and, even with all this going on around her, she did this and asked her mum to get me to do her eulogy at her funeral if the operation failed. On the day we came to celebrate her life, the hardest moment was talking about the life of a young woman, whom we lost so young, with so much to give and to consider all the things she could have done. It was an honour to talk and celebrate her life, as she cast quite a shadow, especially as she was only on the planet for such a short time and spent a third of that time wrestling with the Big C and its side effects. Sharon, 'Quelle courage!', you inspired me, you still inspire me. You always encouraged me Miss Jones and I will always be grateful. Thank you Sharon. She never complained, all the challenges that life threw at her, she took them on. She loved dancing; more than that, she was a dancer and she seemed just to dance on regardless, I hope she is still dancing.

How do you encourage or inspire? Through words or actions? What torch do you carry?

What do you tell yourself each day?

"I am a data entry clerk"

"I am an accountant"

"I am just a housewife"

"I am just a financial adviser"

Do not sell yourself short – look at the greatness that you do. Look at how many people you touch. Is it with flair? Is it with drudgery? It is in your hands. Tomorrow, why don't you try something different (drudgery will always be there, so leave that in the cupboard for another day). Try replacing the phrases above with these:

"~~I am a data entry clerk~~"?

I am a management technician/I play with data all day getting it into the best shape to keep the world turning.

"~~I am an accountant~~"?

I save people tax to make their lives and businesses happier.

"~~I am just a housewife~~"?

I run a team of four who will be the next business leaders, looking after tomorrow. I am needed to make sure they get there/I am responsible for the next Einstein/I am making the best future I can.

"~~I am just a financial adviser~~"?

I help people/I deliver £300,000 cheques/I keep businesses going/ I keep dreams alive/I help people retire in style/I make sure that families are protected..

These are just tweaks but once again this is your movie of your life; you are the director; you are the main star – the film set and extras are all down to you. I would encourage you to make the best movie you can and if you need to change the script then change the script. Don't Settle – Seize!

The great Vince Lombardi said, "It's not whether you get knocked down, it's whether you get up." His field was American football, whilst he was given proper kudos for his many wins and creating that will to win in his team, his advice, like Ali's and like Rocky's (to Adonis Creed in CREED: "It's you – against you") is not confined to sport, it is about life. The events I have done are about stepping up and seeing if I have the minerals. There is no boast in any of this, how can there be? You did read the Team Hoyt Chapter, right? I challenged myself in a way I couldn't imagine, as did Goggins, albeit in very different arenas. However, the point remains: these are personal journeys, just as yours is, so what is your philosophy on your life? Do you test yourself? Do you stretch yourself? Do you get back up?

To underline this, highlight it and bring it home, Vince Lombardi goes on to say: "I would say that the quality of each man's life is the full measure of that man's commitment of excellence and victory – whether it be football, whether it be business, whether it be politics or government or what have you." Picture Ali with that Olympic torch. He seized it. In fact, with all he had going on with his continuing fight against Parkinson's, he not only seized the torch but used it to light the Olympic bowl of fire to start the Games.

. . . .

EXERCISE TIME: FIND YOUR SELF-BELIEF

You know that Ali told everyone again and again, "I am the greatest." Get your own self – belief, your totem, something to live by. Think about your purpose, the thing that makes you – YOU. Is it what you do? Is it what you do for others? Is it what you are going to do? Make it simple, make it memorable – make it yours and repeat, repeat and repeat (while doing your reps in the gym, cooking for the family or waiting for the train/plane, repeat, repeat, repeat). Tell those closest to you.

For example, in my case I told everyone I was going to be an IRONMAN® athlete, even though I couldn't swim the distance. I told them all I was going to go to Drama School and become an actor, even though the chances were stacked against me and I had no money to pay for fees. Back you, believe in you, especially when the world is against you. Get your mantra and repeat until it happens, and what then? Then find your next incantation for your next impossible goal.

THE R.O.C.K.Y ROAD
FOR MUHAMMAD ALI

Rise – Just take a look at the man, not only in the ring where he had to rise many times against the odds to show his greatness, but on the world stage as a conscientious objector and one of the few sporting heroes who brought religion out of the shadows, something that defined him.

Obstacles – Petrified of flying, he got on the plane to the Rome Olympics in 1960 and events were set in motion to bring us the most iconic sports person that has ever been. He changed his name and openly embraced Islam after becoming World Champion. He was unable to fight in arguably his best years, but he came back in spite of this to once again become the champ and on and on.

Choices – Ali had a choice, as we all do, but he chose to speak out, to be counted. He chose to announce that he was the greatest and it is hard to argue with this. Charisma, wit, and joy, Ali was a force of nature. He chose to fight in some circumstances and he chose not to fight in others. It is perhaps the latter choice that defines him for us.

Kaizen – Ali was an intelligent man. You can see this in the ring, the many interviews he gave and also arguing his stance with regards to Vietnam. He studied, read and kept working on himself.

You – If you HAD to call yourself "The Greatest" at anything what would it be? Hold on now, don't just dismiss this; if you HAD to, what would it be? Remember Ali started believing he was the greatest even before he was Olympic or world champion. Belief is key and if you don't believe in you then who will? Perhaps a coach/mentor, but you have to believe in you. Try this for a week: tell yourself every morning, "I am the Greatest ..." Have a think about this and decide what you will be the greatest in for the next 168 hours; that is all, just for 168 hours. See it, believe it and see what happens. I dare you, I double dare you.

. . . .

MUSEUM OF MOMENTUM TOUR

Torch, flame on! Yes Ali still holds that torch up, helping us see, we etch this burning flame onto the MUSEum wall along with the rest of our burgeoning creation. The torch is a metaphor – it is purpose, but not just purpose, it is us daring greatly. We are pushing ourselves to a place we have never been, and we need light. We engage a coach because we need someone to back us, someone to remove obstacles, keep our focus, encourage, nurture and support. Either coach others or take a coach to find new limits. Do not just wander, share your gifts, or make the most of them. Do not die "with the music still in you."

CHAPTER V:
BUSINESS

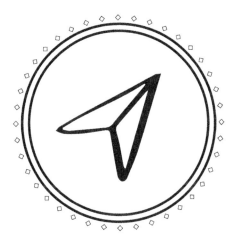

THE WRIGHT
BROTHERS

. . . .

*"If we all worked on the assumption that what is accepted
as true is really true, there would be little hope of advance."*

Orville Wright

Business: The activity of making, buying, selling or supplying goods or services for money.
Work that is part of your job.
Important matters that need to be dealt with or discussed.

....

"If you know what you're worth, then go and get what you're worth but you gotta be willing to take the hits."
Rocky Balboa

I am taking you back over 100 years and talking about business using The Wright Brothers as our ambassadors of business. Why not Branson, Buffett, Gates or Jobs? Partly as you can still see, to this day, the legacy of the Wright Brothers – history is yet to judge our aforementioned brethren. These guys dreamt big and even though the world was saying their dream was impossible, they went and did it anyway. A great first lesson on business I am sure you will agree: dream big. They were not privileged, they did not have an Ivy League education, so no "old school tie"/nepotism rules provided an advantage for Orville and Wilbur. They had no "contacts in the biz," as there was no flying business at the time – THEY CREATED IT.

They made it happen, in spite of their background, education or lack of business "friends." A great second lesson: you can do great things from whatever your vantage point. An interesting point to note is that many successful business folk/entrepreneurs had a rough start in life, did not do well at school, were misunderstood, dyslexic; so it isn't where you start, it is where you finish in this business of life. Lesson three: keep at it. These boys could have folded many times, but they never put the blocks on or, should I say, their way was always "Chocks away!" What is stopping your wheels from turning and hitting the right speed for takeoff?

So what happened to these bicycle repairmen to make them change gear and to look to the skies? It was after the death of Otto Lilienthal in a glider crash in 1896 that the Wright Brothers looked to better designs, inspired by nature (birds). They did this by observing how birds angled their wings for balance in flight in the natural world. (See, that word has come up again. Whether designing or living, balance is all – listen to your Uncle Orville now). Note too when you next get on a plane that all of them are still based on the Wright Brothers original aeronautics.

Can we just take a moment to appreciate their achievements? Orville and Wilbur Wright were not highly trained, much sought-after engineers – they were bicycle repairmen. What took them from running their little bike shop and tinkering with bike frames/wheels and tyres, to being the ones who mastered heavier than air manned flight? Moreover, they took this challenge on when the world was telling them that it was impossible. Do you ever feel like that with your "Business?" Or that you are out of your depth, with a voice saying, "go back to your bikes and leave the world changing stuff to others?" The naysayers are loud and yet still, you persevere, just like the Wright Brothers. Here is a selection of some of the naysayers of their day, who were the respected, educated voices of reason: "Heavier-than-air flying machines are impossible," "I have not the smallest molecule of faith in aerial navigation other than ballooning... I would not care to be a member of the Aeronautical Society," Kelvin, Lord William Thomson 1895 and 1900.

In 1888 Joseph Le Conte, Professor of Geology and Natural History at the University of California, wrote, "I am one of those who think that a flying-machine... is impossible, in spite of the testimony of the birds," (Popular Science Monthly 1884). In 1901, George W. Melville, Chief Engineer of the United States Navy, said, "I am one of those who think that a flying-machine is impossible, in spite of the testimony of the birds." Then there was Simon Newcomb, a fierce impossible-ist even as late as 1906, who wrote in Harper, "The demonstration that no possible combination of known substances, known forms of machinery, and known forms of force can be united in a practicable machine by which men shall fly long distances through the air, seems to the writer as complete as it is possible for the demonstration of any physical fact to be."

The naysayers said it was impossible but the Wright Brothers went and did it. Whatever that thing is that you can "see" but others can't, keep at it; you must keep at it. This book is not a silver bullet on how to run a successful business; the books stores are full of the "next best/hot-selling" book to do that. Like motivation, starting a business and running a successful business comes from within, you need to have faith and like our Brothers here, oftentimes blind faith. Once you believe in yourself, if you want to run a successful business, work hard and surround yourself with the right people, staff and clients; it's as easy as that. For those starting out, you could do a lot worse than investing in, *Start with Why*[26] by Simon Sinek. Sinek talks about the golden circle (inspired by The Golden Ratio (GR) which has preoccupied artists and scientists alike since time immemorial). People have looked to the GR for order, for something formulaic to make more sense of the world around us and our place in it. Put simply, Sinek's "Why" in the dead centre of his Golden Circle is the starting point.

"What is your why?" I hear you say. "What is your *why* behind this book?" Initially it was to document the journey, as I had taken on some things that were impossible to me. I am a husband, father and business owner with many people reliant on me and yet I have done X, Y and Z, and raised tens of thousands for charities. I had to document this, so that when I looked back I would know it wasn't a dream.

Read all the books, go on all the courses you want, but the bottom line is work hard and love what you do. I am in the life business and what I mean by that is that, "I like life" and so I find it necessary to help others. I help people, I always have and always will; it must be chemical as it is something that I don't have a choice in. I was not born into a wealthy family (at least not in the financial sense), I was not blessed with siblings but I have been lucky in a sense that I have chosen whom I call brother and sister. So, on the premise that you too are in this

[26] Simon Sinek, (2009), *Start With Why: How Great Leaders Inspire Everyone To Take Action*, Portfolio

kind of business and enjoy life, press on, the following puts into clear perspective where the balance should be.

....

THE FISHERMAN AND THE BUSINESSMAN

The parable of the fisherman and the businessman shows perspective. The businessman on holiday with his beachside vantage point observes the local fisherman doing his early morning daily catch. The fisherman catches enough fish to feed his family and he rests for the day, he isn't out at sea (working all hours), as he makes time to spend with his family and play with his kids. He even gets to spend time with his friends in the evening playing guitar and celebrating another day, before getting up early and doing it all again. Rather than noticing the balance, the businessman advises the fisherman to scale up, to work longer hours, get a bigger boat, employ more people. He looks for efficiencies and ways to build a bigger and better business (from his perspective), but the end result of all those labour intensive hours and increased risk is exactly where the humble fisherman is now. The businessman is perhaps one of the biggest in his commercial world, but the fisherman is not only a fisherman; he is a parent, a friend who also fishes. Balance is all.

How is your balance – are you out to sea too often, are you able to play with your kids everyday? And what about your friends, what is your version of being a success and a good friend and family member? Have you ever considered it or has life got in the way? This or that deadline, that end of tax year report.

What is success? What does it mean? What does it mean to you? Is it the money? Is it the time? Is it being with your family? Is it being clever? Or is it being alive? – you decide.

....

THE LESSON OF "KNOWING" WHERE TO HIT

A ship engine fails on its maiden voyage and no one can fix it. They call for an expert, and one who has been in the ship fixing business for 40 years duly arrives. After inspecting the engine very carefully, top to bottom, the expert reaches into their bag and pulls out a hammer. They gently tap something and instantly, the engine lurches into life. The engine is fixed!

Seven days later the ship owners get the expert's bill for £10,000. "What?!" the owner says, "You hardly did anything, send us an itemized bill." The reply simply says:

Tapping with a hammer: £2

Knowing where to tap: £9,998

Don't underestimate your experience to date. Here endeth the lesson!

ROCKY FILENAME	
THE WRIGHT BROTHERS Orville Wright & Wilbur Wright	
OCCUPATION	Bicycle Repairmen
MADE THEIR ENTRANCE	(OW) 19th August 1871, Dayton, Ohio, US (WW) 16th April 1867, Millville, Indiana, US
TOOK THEIR LAST BOW	(OW) 30th January 1948 Dayton, Ohio, US (WW) 30th May 1912 Dayton, Ohio, US
EDUCATION	Dayton Central High School
AKA	The Wright Brothers The Fathers of Modern Aviation
ACHIEVEMENTS (SOME OF..)	1892 Opened their own bicycle shop 1896 Designed their own 'safer' bicycle 1903 Created the 'The Wright Flyer of 1903' first successful airplane flight on December 17, 1903 in Kitty Hawk, North Carolina.

At the same time that Orville and Wilbur were using nature/ birds to evolve us into creatures that could achieve flight, Langley was commissioned for the same purpose; a competitor, a nemesis or the stone to sharpen themselves on? Samuel Pierpont Langley had government funding and had connections as the secretary of the Smithsonian. Langley was well educated and was given at least $100,000 to make his Aerodrome fly. His version though was only able to launch through catapult and the pilot was unable to steer. It was only eight days after his spectacular failure on launch that the Wright Brothers, who by comparison were poorly educated, without the friends, connections or sponsors Langley had, and with a budget of circa $1,000, mastered take off and landing. The rest, as they say, is history or rather today as their designs and data analysis is still used... Perhaps even the future? Whereas poor Langley, who perhaps equally coveted the title of the Father of Modern Aviation, became a footnote on how not to do it. The Wrights succeeded as they let their dreams lead them and then used the real-world data that they observed in nature to make their dream a reality.

Langley however, had an idea, a fixed point, and like King Canute was trying to control nature rather than embrace it. Why mention this? You aren't a cutting-edge designer wannabe, so what? This happened over 100 years ago. True, it was many moons past, but what are you doing about your dreams? Are you using nature or thrashing against it looking for a different result? Are you catapulting into the sky only to crash down, not evaluating what you have learned? Do you revisit where it went wrong and finesse it, OR just keep launching and getting the same results? Is there something so simple yet so revolutionary, such as a bird's wing, that could change your trajectory, how you soar through the sky or will you continually blast through and not learn?

The wisdom of the Wrights' is that they learnt from their mistakes; they failed and they learned from it. More than this, when the world was telling them it was impossible, they kept dreaming and they kept at it. Whatever the world is telling you, just keep at it. We talk about bees and that it should be impossible for them to fly. Gravity is telling them they can't fly, many scientists and learned folk say that they can't fly – fortunately the bee does not hear them, or doesn't listen. The bee says, "Can't talk right now (or is that Wright now?) I have just got to fly over to those flowers, excuse me." We will hear that the bee thing is a myth and science knows oh so much, but bringing it back to the Wright Brothers, we know that to fly takes effort and ingenuity. How many bees did it take to learn to fly in "their way," using oscillation to still fly with their fat bodies and little wings, even though all around them is yelling at them (as with the Wright Brothers) it is impossible.

Let us choose for ourselves what is impossible. Be careful who you listen to out there; if the Wright Brothers had listened we may still be on boats and the globalisation of the world may not have happened. Be careful too what you say to folk; if you find yourself with your impossible mic turned on and arguing that it is impossible, that someone can't do something, that it is beyond them, take a step back and mute the mic. Let us all fly in our own way. Yes, there are dangers but what do you want to do, soar or be a bore? Enjoy where your and others' potential can take you or them, or just say, "Nah, tried it, didn't work." When it gets dark and you are about to give up, just think about those brothers who came from nothing and made the impossible possible. They didn't let anyone stop them dreaming. Believe that you too have the Wright stuff. Following this theme, we say thanks to Richard Bach (author of *Illusions*) who, whilst soaring up there in his biplane with auto mechanic Donald Shimoda, a reluctant Messiah, learns, "Argue for your limitations and sure enough they're yours." It was 1998 when this simple line arrived with me and hasn't left me since. It is a truism – WE define/limit ourselves, as equally as we have the power to elevate ourselves and others, you choose.

. . . .

THE ROAD NOT TAKEN

Two roads diverged in a yellow wood,
And sorry I could not travel both
And be one traveler, long I stood
And looked down one as far as I could
To where it bent in the undergrowth;
Then took the other, as just as fair,
And having perhaps the better claim,
Because it was grassy and wanted wear;
Though as for that the passing there
Had worn them really about the same,
And both that morning equally lay
In leaves no step had trodden black.
Oh, I kept the first for another day!
Yet knowing how way leads on to way,
I doubted if I should ever come back.
I shall be telling this with a sigh

Somewhere ages and ages hence:
Two roads diverged in a wood, and I—
I took the one less traveled by,
And that has made all the difference.
(Robert Frost)

There will always be that "other" road. You have to take the road that takes you to where you want to go and if there isn't a road then make one. Too often we blame circumstance, lack of opportunity or luck and to a degree they all have a part to play, but we have to create our own luck. We are the rainmakers, all too often though we give someone else the power to decide. If you want to be the best salesperson, manager, philanthropist, parent, lover – just decide.

"If I can change, you can change, then everybody can change" (Rocky IV). Change is just a state of mind. Most of us don't respond well to change, while others embrace it and the rest strive for it. We have to have the vision, we have to see it and walk towards it and keep walking. Just like with the challenges previously mentioned there was a start line and a finishing line. Before you start, see yourself across the finishing line. See it and add as much detail as you can – the smile on your face, the people around you, the noise, the smells, the feeling – and you are mostly there. This comes from the man who went from being a very podgy child who thought running wasn't his thing, to doing half marathons without training and coming in with a respectable time. I have changed, my body has changed, but it is my mind that takes me there.

How can you apply this back story to your life to affect your future, your relationships, your career, your legacy? The answer is simple, see it. But be clear about that vision. So many business owners have been very successful with their business and this was their focus, but when they get the letter from their wife's solicitor it is too late and all that they were building, and the people they were building it for, have gone. Do they still feel successful? Be clear and take the family with you.

....

iROCKY

THE "M6 MOMENT"

Many years ago, while travelling to coach advisers in Stoke, I had my "M6 moment." My kids were young and as a parent, you know you need to enjoy this time as they grow so fast. I loved all of it: the nappy changing, the feed times, the school runs, the bedtime stories and being the one who they would always fall asleep on. Yet here I was travelling at dawn to work with these unmotivated advisers. The advisers were there because they had to be there, they were employees, rather than people investing in themselves because they wanted more and to be more. I was leaving my family for this? If you aren't around much, missing those big family times or even the humdrum times, just like sitting down to dinner and catching up on each other's day, is a big deal. How much is keeping you away from home and/or your family? What is your number/

paycheque, to keep you on the road? One of the main lessons from Tony Hsieh's book *Delivering Happiness*[27] is: you have to sit at the right table and surround yourself with the right people – simple in mind, easy in practice? I realised you have to work with those you want to, for me that is those who are forward driven. This was my life and I didn't like where I was going so you know what? I decided I was going to change it!

Surely there is no finer table than the dinner table with your family; if you feel that there is, then you may well want to have a word with yourself. You can have those A+ business types around you and you are earning a gazillion dollars, but if at the end of the day you aren't going to celebrate that with your nearest and dearest – really, what is it all for? Moving and shaking A+ type people will come and go, you will make some money, you will lose some money; but your family, your partner, your children are always there, a constant. They are your time and your legacy so make them a massive part of your business and your success.

Back to the M6. It is the longest motorway in the UK at 230 miles, it also boasts Spaghetti Junction. It was while driving on this motorway that I had my "moment" and decided to take "the road less travelled and that has made all the difference now" (thank you Robert Frost). There would be no six bedrooms, four kids and stay at home mum while I was jumping from employed role to employed role, not fulfilling my potential,

---

[27] Tony Hsieh, (2010), *Delivering Happiness: A Path to Profits, Passion and Purpose*, Grand Central Publishing

investing it in improving the skill set of those who don't want to transform, but just want to be comfortable. As we know there was no magic there. The comfort zone is like an island, where we happily maroon ourselves and our dreams and "get by" until we are old and grey and blame everything, and everyone else, that we haven't achieved! No, I decided to start my own practice, dance to my own tune and invest time in those who truly wanted coaching, those wanting to improve, those who wanted to take action.

. . . .

IRONMAN® UK (BOLTON 2019)

What can we learn from failure? Business, personal it doesn't matter – it has a gift for you. I took on Bolton with very little training, as I had become an Ultra runner that year, trusting mostly to muscle memory, but not much time out on the bike. As a triathlete you have three disciplines and you cannot skip any of them or you are risking disappointment, and disappointment is what I got. The 2.4-mile swim went okay, I was out of the lake in under 90 mins and on to the bike. The course was two loops of a new, and dare I say brutal course. I have never seen so many bikes on the roadside and a DNF rate of circa 35 per cent (I believe that they have now changed the route!). I did the first loop, took on all those hills and the descents (with those sharp dogleg turns), but what I didn't give full respect to was that there was an additional cut off time at the 92 mile point, even though I still had an hour left at mile 90 the marshall drove alongside and retired me. I was incensed, but what lesson is there in this failure? Call it unfinished business, I couldn't let that be my IRONMAN® triathlon swan song. Instead I used the pain of that experience and signed up for another three long-distance triathlons! Grrrrrrrrrrr!

We cannot be defined by our failures, only by how we react to them. I hear that Japanese wisdom, reminding me "Fall down seven times get up eight." What can we learn when we fall? We all fall at some point don't we, but do we learn from it? That's what is key, not to wallow in Failureville, licking our wounds and picking at all those old scars, opening up the wounds because we like to be reminded of the pain. We have to show our scars as a badge of honour, a demonstration of defiance. To bring this back to our chapter header: business, show me a businessperson who has not failed. All the best ones have, but rather than this failure taking them down it became a bedrock for them to stand on. It is okay to fail, just as knowing your *why* is important to get you through the tough times, knowing *why* you failed makes you better and stronger.

I failed in Bolton because I casually ignored another cut off time, I had already done the bike course once and it was with only 20 miles to go that the marshall said I was cut. There's gung ho and there's foolish – I was being foolhardy, do I learn from this or yearn from this? Disrespect it or introspect it? Did I curl up in my shell or rewind and show up again, knowing that the extra imposed cut off time could be a problem, and therefore blast the swim and not dance around in the transition.

Like Jane Tomlinson (more from her later) and my little cousin at IRONMAN® France, I now knew what it felt like to be dismissed or denied that exhilaration of crossing the line. I had earned a DNF – did not finish.

Do not take defeat lightly, let it forge you. Use the pain; I am currently looking at doing seven more IRONMAN® races before I hang up my triathlon boots and one is an IRONMAN® full distance plus 12 per cent! So put that in your pipe and smoke it Bolton! My ambition will not stay on your course for long. Although initially despondent, I couldn't blame anybody but myself. It was on me, but that turned to fire in my belly, the phoenix rising. The key lesson here was I was flying solo without a coach, without a training regime and thought I could just knock this one out (big mistake). Let us agree that you need a coach to do one of these things justice. I had decided not to proceed with my coach on this occasion – she was/is ace, but I had a family member suffering from depression and wanted to "be there" for her when she needed me and not beat myself up that I had missed training sessions as they backed up and up. In the grand scheme of things, my thinking was that my coach may make me quicker by 30-40 minutes, but being needed at home for that hour or two, or ten, would be better spent. That's the first lesson: use a coach. Don't misunderstand, I took the foundations we had built together and used them as my platform, but I could not spend as much time on this.

Even if you have run across a desert, the race doesn't know that. You like to help people; so what? The race doesn't care. Each time we stand on a start line (sport, business, parent) we have to perform, we have to get across the line we said we would, or it makes a mockery of even standing on the start line in the first place.

Check out Derek Redmond at the 1992 Olympics in Barcelona. He was tipped as the potential Gold medallist in the 400 metres, Bang! The starter pistol goes off for the race and the athletes begin. Redmond is looking good and then halfway through the race, he hears another bang, and that was his hamstring. He knew how bad it was straight away. He knew that there would never be an Olympic opportunity like this for him again, tears come, of pain and frustration, and as the reality dawns that this is it for him, he starts limping/hopping. The race is over, all the competitors are done but Redmond keeps going, he wants to get across the line, it's all he has thought about/dreamt about for the last four years, that line. He limps and is clearly in significant pain. The race officials try to stop him, his Dad breaks through the crowd and on to the running track, he shoos the race officials away (putting it nicely, check out the race on YouTube[28], you'll go through a myriad of emotions from pain to exhilaration). Redmond limps his way across the line. His race is run; a damaged hamstring, insistent race officials – nothing was going to stop him.

Think about your obstacles for a moment, one of which might even be you, just like Redmond's hamstring. It might be "officials" telling you you can't do something and who have you

[28] Just4realng, *Derek Redmond Never Give Up*, YouTube, available at: www.youtube.com/watch?v=A9GWhSndmf0

got to lean on and get you to where you want to be? Is that obstacle a real obstacle? Bolton could have been that for me – it beat me and I am done. I went back to the lab though, looked deep within myself, and was honest with myself. After that regroup I came back stronger, not defeated, ready to go again and go further. That obstacle you chose, do a deep dive and be honest – is it you? If so, what habits do you need to change so that the obstacles – like those I faced in Bolton and like all those failed businesses behind ALL successful business people – become something to stand on, to work through to make you stronger and get you to the next level?

EXERCISE TIME:
YOUR DEFINITIVE TO-DO LIST

Write a to-do list, but one that you will do. IT WILL BE DONE. Don't just fill a page with, take business to £ million net income, get fitter etc. Put things on the list that you will do. If it is a daily list, they must *all* be done that day. If it is a weekly list, they must *all* be completed that week. For a monthly to-do list... you get the idea.

By writing it down in pen, it subconsciously becomes a contract and by committing to only putting things down that not only need to get done, but will get done will guarantee your business gets more successful and this is true not only for a professional business, but also the business of YOU.

A note of encouragement: Ten years ago I was bracing myself for the London to Paris cycle and now, ten years later as I write this, I am prepping for my third IRONMAN® event in three months, with the last one chalked up only three weeks previously – it's impossible, or is it? When I look back, what has been achieved in those ten years, 98 per cent of people would have thought impossible: buy your new home for cash? Buy another business? It really is a wonderful life and you can design it – just remind yourself of what you took from impossible to possible. It just takes two letters ("I" and "M") or even just build some space around you (I'm possible).

THE R.O.C.K.Y ROAD
FOR THE WRIGHT BROTHERS

Rise – The boys had a simple dream, no one had done it before. They were the originals of 'Rise'. How do we get up there? How can we control it? How can we get back down? The birds have it – the answer is in nature.

Obstacles – Little funding and a popular explosion of scientists and dreamers working on being the first. They supported each other as "family," they dreamed big and they kept dreaming even when some of the best minds of the time were telling them it was impossible.

Choices – They could have decided to listen to the naysayers and pack it all up, and go and fix a few more bikes. The simple life calls to us all.

Kaizen – They chose not to listen to anyone's voice but their own. They learnt from their failures, the crashes and literally took off. Perfecting their aerodynamics and using nature as a template, they worked and worked and against the odds gave us manned flight. That achievement though, that greatness, could easily have died with them if they had given up in the face of all the noise against them and, as Thoreau reminds us, "The mass of men lead lives of quiet desperation, and go to the grave with the song still in them." They stayed the course, they believed in what they were creating and here we are, singing their song for them/with them.

You – Do you believe in your project? Do you believe in your business, whatever that may be? Do you believe so much that when people laugh at you, you continue on, in spite of that noise? There are people who fix bikes and then there are bike fixers who can fly – it is a choice. In 1957, Laika, in Sputnik 2, orbited the Earth. Only some 54 years after the Wright Brothers said, "Yes you can fly" there was a dog sitting in a rocket going around the globe and you still don't believe in pushing back the boundaries of "the possible." How far do we have to go with this?

. . . .

MUSEUM OF MOMENTUM TOUR

We are here on our fifth visit – you stand and our fifth place is filled by the Wright Brothers. They are asking what happened to that dream of yours? That business you were always going to set up, but is now buried deep. What will help you take flight, grow wings and realise that dream? To be successful in business you need a dream/vision, it has to drive you. If you are without the funding, support and the thousand other obstacles we put in our way, remember it is your dream and trust that your drive will pull you through.

When the world is telling you it is impossible or that you do not have the Wright stuff, obsess until your wheels have left the ground. Come on, if poorly educated bicycle repairmen can reinvent the art of possible, then what is holding you back from doing the same with your dream/business? You know the story of Icarus, flying too close to the sun and the wax holding his wings together melting? Well, the warning to us from *The Icarus Deception* by Seth Godin is not the danger of flying too close to the sun; the danger is flying too low, not achieving the giddy heights that you could reach; but arriving at mediocrity as your best outcome. We get comfortable, we stop dreaming and our feet stay firmly on terra firma with our dream/our treasure buried somewhere deep in that terra firma. It's that old adage of not aiming too high and missing, but aiming too low and hitting. The Wright Brothers are sitting at the table here telling you that you can, "If we can, you can. You can. You can. You can. You can. You can. You can."

CHAPTER VI

CHALLENGE

WINSTON
CHURCHILL

. . . .

"Continuous effort — not strength or intelligence — is the key to unlocking our potential"[29]

Winston Churchill

[29] Blenheim Partners, 'Sir Winston Churchill – Perspectives on Leadership', available at: blenheimpartners.com/wp-content/uploads/2013/10/Sir-Winston-Churchill-Perspectives-on-Leadership.pdf

Challenge: a new or difficult task that tests somebody's ability and skill.

. . . .

Churchill has more than 1,000 biographies on his life. There is little for me to add about the man, but he can add to us, even now. It is through his qualities of determination in the face of adversity that we have included him as one of our ambassadors for The R.O.C.K.Y Project. In recent years he has become somewhat controversial, as we cast our righteous, all knowing 21st century eyes over the postmortem on the man, his actions and character. We strive though to focus on the best, on the gift he has for us. As Shakespeare has Mark Anthony, say in his Julius Caesar (Act III Scene II), "The evil that men do lives after them, the good is oft interred in their bones." So let us look at the good today, "Friends, Rockys and Countrymen lend me your ears..."

ROCKY FILENAME

CHURCHILL
Sir Winston Leonard Spencer Churchill

OCCUPATION	Prime Minister Journalist & Writer
MADE THEIR ENTRANCE	30th November 1874, Blenheim Palace, Oxfordshire
TOOK THEIR LAST BOW	24th January 1965, London
EDUCATION	Harrow The Royal Military College
AKA	Churchill Bulldog
ACHIEVEMENTS	Prime Minister 1940-1945 & 1951-1955 1953 Nobel Prize for Literature 1895 Joined The Royal Cavalry as soldier and part-time journalist 1899 elected Conservative MP for Oldham 1904 Defected to The Liberal Party/Government eventually becoming The First Lord of the Admiralty. He resigned from this position and travelled to the Western Front to fight. The interwar years saw Churchill again 'cross the floor' from the Liberals back to the Conservative Party. 1924 Chancellor Of The Exchequer 1929 Lost his seat

ACHIEVEMENTS CONTINUED	1940 Prime Minister of a coalition Government. Churchill also adopted the self-created position of Minister for Defence.

Being brought up mostly by my Grandparents in the '70s there was still that sense of gratitude, even familiarity, with Churchill. Like most, my Grandfather never spoke about his time serving in the War. My Nan would talk about what it was like at home in Warwick though and the "spirit," and it is on this that I wish to speak with you about Churchill.

Churchill was aged 65 when WWII broke out – surely he should have been focusing on "getting his affairs in order" rather than becoming Prime Minister and being the lonely voice in stopping the impending new world order? He had a speech impediment; however, he is renowned as one of the best orators of all time. He made many mistakes on his way to "our darkest hour" but he did not remain in the shadows and be defined by getting it wrong. Surely his legacy to us is that we all make mistakes – and we will continue to make mistakes and we all have things going against us, some inherent and some self-inflicted – but we can still rise up and we can take people with us. And we can do this at any age!

With that in mind, armed with his doggedness and pledge, "I have nothing to offer but blood, toil, tears and sweat," (13th May 1940); pack your suitcases as we visit Norway and Wales for some character building through challenge: Trial by Iron!

iROCKY

WHAT IS YOUR WHY? (IRONMAN®
NORWAY AND IRONMAN® WALES 2018)

HEART RATE MONITOR MUSINGS (26.1.18)

Back in my young heady days, I thought that Training Zones and heart rate monitors were just gear for the sake of having gear, but that all changed in 2017 when I trained for IRON-MAN® Nice, in a way I had never trained for anything before. I found the benefits of staying in my comfort zone, moreover I learned what happened to my body when I left it, and what drive and force I needed to get to a higher level. For those who are uninitiated in the ways of the zone, here you go:

Zone 1: Super easy effort, working only at 20-30 per cent of your potential, keeping your heart rate below 70 per cent of it's maxwork rate.

Zone 2: This is still at an easy, conversational pace. Your workrate is between 40-50 per cent and your good old heart is around 70-85 per cent.

Zone 3: This is a restricted zone, otherwise referred to as the danger zone. You don't tend to spend lots of time here or if you do, watch out for injury or prolonged recovery periods of time in this zone. You tend to be working at 60-70 per cent effort and your heart rate is bouncing around 85-95 per cent.

Zone 4: This is your threshold zone, your legs and lungs will burn, you are flat out; all out you can only live here for up to an hour. The effort you are working at is between 80-90 per cent and your subsequent heart rate is beating at around 95 per cent.

Do I hear a, "So what?" The point being made here is that if you spend too long on your comfort zone and don't stretch it, you don't go anywhere; in fact the inherent fitness that you had starts to dissipate. If you try and live in Zone 4, well you die. What is the wisdom here? Our flow state uses all four zones and taking this out of a fitness metaphor for a moment; just think about your life, how do you function? Where do you sit in these zones? If you were wearing a heart monitor for your job how much time would you spend in each zone? Are you sleepwalking through your day, or stepping it up some? How about in relationships? Is it all too easy for you, you could have this relationship in your sleep with minimal effort, or are you investing more energy working on it, increasing the intensity of the relationship and its subsequent longevity?

Ask yourself, are you a fierce friend, or a part-timer? Think about how you function on a daily, monthly or annual basis — where do you sit? How much effort are you applying to your life or are you melted into your coach, your phone, your social media digital; self touching a screen, but not touching lives and just being a voyeur on your own life? Step it up and see what happens! You will surprise yourself, but you have to keep at it, don't try it and then go into tourist mode again. This is your life, get the pulse racing some!

Bouncing you now back in time:

It is 2018, January 25th to be precise, only four days before my Goddaughter becomes 18; Oh Lord, that has gone by in a blink! The last "event" of mine was IRONMAN® Weymouth 70.3, in September 2017. With the exception of running with a friend in the Stratford-upon-Avon half marathon at the last minute (unfortunately her running partner, my good lady wife, picked up an injury), I had done nothing for the body. Instead I was focusing on my consultancy business, taking more exams and graduating as a Registered Life Planner. Run, bike, swim? All my kit was put in a box for me to focus on other things non-tri-athlon. Why do I mention this? Well because today, I decided to go for a little run, to start in earnest for my biggest year of IRONMAN® events – The Outlaw 70.3 (20.5.18), IRONMAN® Norway (1.7.18) and the prize of IRONMAN® Wales (9.9.18). I had also registered my interest for the Marathon Des Sables (MdS) in 2019. Please don't ask why, my family asked and I couldn't give them an answer, other than whilst my body can, I would like to take on the hardest challenges and can rest on "the old bench" when I am old.

Why bring my heart rate monitor into this? Because this little run of mine was tough all round, but I was armed with my Christmas present: a Garmin 920Xt with accompanying heart rate monitor. I saw my heart's journey, as we began to get rid of the cobwebs and start moving towards Nottingham, Haugesund and Tenby respectively. It got me thinking that if we were to wear a heart monitor that could measure if we are living with our heart, or rather on purpose, wouldn't that be a good thing, in relationships as well as in business? What about if you could see when you are working too hard at something, or not working hard enough? Athletes use heart rate monitors to measure their performance all the time. How could we, mere mortals, measure our life performance? I think we can and, by the way, I am not saying let us just live using our hearts, hearts on our sleeves, impetuously, no. What I am saying is that if our heart is the motor, the centre, the drive; let's get it in the right gear and use it proportionately. Too often we invest our time in the wrong people and not "on purpose."

. . . .

on purpose intentionally, deliberate, consciously, premeditatedly.

. . . .

Too often we don't check in with ourselves on how we are doing and ask whether we are giving it our all.

The lesson from this is that I am going to wear a monitor, a life monitor, to help me see when I am exerting myself in a less worthy cause and need to save my energy, and focus on those that do truly need me. Otherwise you will burn up, you will not have the necessary energy for the tasks that demand more than your comfort zone, or zone one. You cannot sleepwalk from one crisis, or challenge, to another. You would not put as much time, energy and resource to a 5K run as you would a marathon, so you need to allocate and monitor to ensure that if and when the challenge comes you can answer it. That is called living deliberately.

. . . .

IRONMAN® NORWAY (30TH JUNE 2018)

This was the first time they were doing an IRONMAN® 140.6 race in Norway. Look at those hills, the gradients, the pain, the map, as they say in NLP circles, is not the territory. My advice? Do not do a long-haul flight just before the race! Additionally, do not get a cold/flu/bug on said plane. I was so good – I kept hydrated and had a good sleep – yet in the early hours of the 30th I felt that I was only one hour away from bailing and getting a DNS (Did Not Start) after my name. Ironically, even though I didn't perform spectacularly with the travel and had a bug against me, there were many for IRONMAN® Norway who didn't make the start line; I am once again reminded of one of my favourite quotes from Theodore Roosevelt: "The credit goes to the man in the arena..."

It seemed as though all the "very" Iron folk had gathered in Haugesund for the very first full-distance IRONMAN® Norway. There were only 600 or so people on the planet who accepted the challenge, with only 532 getting across the line. There was the lure of 30 Kona places – these are much coveted and on most "must do" lists for IRONMAN® race aspirants. It felt like we had turned up to the Olympics and we were the dart players (based on mine and my little cousin's shape as well as the gear we had brought – it felt like we had brought darts to an archery competition) so out of our depth were we. The chap I sat next to for the mandatory briefing on the Saturday morning had only done IRONMAN® Boulder several weeks back and had already got a Kona slot but had booked IRON-MAN® Norway previously to guarantee his place in Hawaii (the birthplace of IRONMAN® triathlons in 1978). You get an idea of the crowd.

I had to go to the pharmacy and get some magic Norwegian paracetamol and Ibuprofen – I was in bad shape having picked up a nasty bug. Mindfulness to the rescue and that pain relief (just so you know I do not take tablets; I need to be in a bad state to consider them. I perhaps had taken four paracetamol tablets over the previous four years). Not a bit of it in Norway, I needed something and needed it now! Meditation came to my aid as well. I was unable to sleep the night before the race so I focused on my breath and considered how I could swim front crawl, all bunged up. The obstacles were flying at me, I was weak but then a vision came to me. It looked like a massive old hall and there was something comforting or reassuring about it. In the middle raged a massive fire and the smoke was carried up through a hole in the middle of the roof. Somehow, I got strength from it. No Jane Tomlinson (as you will hear more on) or fear of the unknown to get me through this one, in fact I was approaching this in an almost cavalier style, which I hasten to add is not the way! RESPECT THE DISTANCE is the WAY.

I made it to the marathon stage and, looking at the 17 hour cut off, felt this could be close. Why am I here, I asked myself? What is my why? Then I remembered that I told my kids I was coming here to do this and if I now didn't do it:

A. That is telling them I planned to fail as I didn't train hard

B. I hadn't seen my little ones for a couple of weeks – I had to come back with a medal

C. My grandfather, when we played chess together said, "You play your game always" and so I did. Not quite hearing the fanfare, I mustered up some strength and began to run and was very happy with the last mile in sight.

It was still very light when I finished, but I couldn't make out any faces in the crowd through the tears. I built up to the now ritualised Bibb sprint finish. This is a habit which was started by my eldest daughter Meg during her cross country at primary school, and all of us have brought it to each race since. I crossed the line, although not jumping up and dancing as only 50 per cent of the team had succeeded. I used the mandatory Rocky pose to signify that the race was over, got my silver blanket and had the promise of some food (although Norway only offered beefburgers, so being the token vegetarian of the race I had to make do with the pricey beer to start the healing process).

My little cousin found me and told me that he did the swim and bike, but narrowly missed the cut off time. I started kicking myself for listening to him at T1 when he came out of the water and shouted "Balboa!" and we were both thinking this is game on! I offered to get his bag for a quick transition, but him being the better cyclist he said no and waved me on, saying he would catch me up on the bike, but that was never to be. I left him behind and for that I will keep beating myself up, until he does get across that line and hears those immortal words, "You are an IRONMAN®!"

Here is the report I sent back to my Tri Club (Cov Tri otherwise known as "The Spots" for their stand out kit):

REPORT BACK ON IRONMAN©
Norway to Coventry Tri Club (July 2018)

On Norway and the race... you quickly discover that Norway is beautiful, right from the flight in. The swim is in a lake, but they were able to put lanes in so it was fairly straight forward, as someone who had an inherent fear of swimming and on one of his early Olympic races had to give a competitor mouth-to-mouth (in the Thames), this came back to me as soon as I hit the water. I couldn't really breath well because of this flu and it got right in my head. 2.4 miles felt an awfully long way and so I breast stroked for the first 300 metres and was thinking about calling it a day. However, thanks to all the swim coaches at Cov Tri – particularly Mark and Tony for their encouragement when I started in the Cov Tri pool in November 2016 and couldn't front crawl – I dug deep and reminded myself that I could do this and have done it before. I must have enjoyed myself out there as my Garmin tells me I did an extra 300 metres! On to the bike; they said "rolling hills," but perhaps that's Norwegian for gruelling. One competitor was muttering under his breath that he had counted 215 hills! As I am never going to win one of these, I stopped to help a competitor BAOZ from Israel who was in trouble and I pumped up his tyre. I completed the cycle and got to the T2 only minutes before the ten-hour cut off time. On to the run, which goes by the harbourside in Haugesund *and where you pass the finishing line eight times! As I didn't see my cousin on the run laps I knew that his race had ended and I had so wanted him to get across the line. As the time ticked by I thought of stopping but I told my kids I was going to do this and didn't want to let them down. I hobbled on and got across the line in 15:56 – the cut off time was 16 hours 30 mins. There were only 600 competitors, but from all over, and as there were 30 Kona slots up for grabs most of the field were tasty with only a couple of weekend warriors like me on the start line. Would I recommend this one – yes, as the views on the bike were outstanding. I could have saved at least 20 minutes on my swim and I am sure if I was able to train for this one, and had not had the conference in the States just before, I could have better represented. The marathon just seemed to go on forever, but that was partly because I was just gutted for my little cousin as we started this journey together and instead of elation at the end, we just cried into our VERY EXPENSIVE Norwegian beer. It is worth noting for those who are considering this event that Norway is THE most expensive country in the world and when you are trying to console someone with a pint that cost £14, you do make sure you finish your beer! Even if you couldn't make sure they finished the race.*

Three quarters of the way through the ride and after my wobble in the lake, the question 'WHY?' kept coming back time and time again. Bigger still, why was I doing IRONMAN® Wales in nine weeks if I was feeling like this? IRONMAN®

Wales is arguably one of the hardest IRONMAN® races out there! Amazingly with this sport, when you think you have had enough, you get across the line and say no more. Then you recover almost immediately and start thinking it wasn't too bad! IRONMAN® Wales bring it!

. . . .

IRONMAN® WALES (9TH SEPTEMBER 2018)

As with the London Marathon in 2000, this was going to be my last full-distance IRONMAN®, regarded as one of the toughest or *the* toughest, depending on which weather turns up. My little cousin drives from Edinburgh – my cornerman, chalking up three countries to get me to the start line; after seeing my state after IRONMAN® Norway, a part of him had to see this to believe it. What I didn't know was that my Mum and wife would surprise me on the start line! I don't ask people to take time out and come to cheer me on, as I am not the fastest and it will be a long day for them, but I see my loved ones in the crowd all the time. I carry them with me, see them and hear them – they are never far from me. There were more people in my corner than I could have expected or deserve, they know it would be a long day and they rallied to help me get across the line. Taking on The Dragon comes with a larger fear factor, the rough sea, the jellyfish, the hills on the 12-mile bike ride, the hills on the marathon! Joseph Campbell talks about 'dragons', often as a big part of our world myth culture[30]. However, the dragon represents us. We are the hero on the journey but we are also the toughest adversary we have to overcome; we are the dragon, the toughest obstacle. Like Luke Skywalker (in Star Wars: The Empire Strikes Back) entering the cave and fighting and beating the spectre of Darth Vader, only to see part of Vader's mask shatter revealing Luke's own face; oftentimes we are fighting ourselves. We are shadow boxing the silhouette of our very self. Can you see anything of this in you?

The dragon for me represents that part of us that doesn't want to fail. We all have a trait inside us that wants to overcome, to succeed, but the fear of not succeeding manifests itself as a dragon. It is always waiting in the pit of your stomach, waiting for the fall and devouring all the inspiration, time, sacrifices and great intentions invested for your latest challenge. The dragon ahead of me was all about my belief that I would rise rather than fall and even though I felt I was on the cliff ledge I couldn't let doubt enter and start trying to pull my fingers off the ledge, one my one. I had to hold fast and know that to climb you do need to let go to reach up. Let's be frank, I had winged IRONMAN® France and IRONMAN® Norway and now I was to beat the Dragon in Wales. I had to recognise the dragon part of me, what was inside of me holding me back and what better place than the land of the dragon – Wales. I kept telling myself, I can do this, I can take it on, it is me against me, fear and doubt do not play a part here. I'm going vertical,

---

30 Joseph Campbell, (2014), *The Hero's Journey: Joseph Campbell on His Life and Work*, New World Library, 3rd edition

I am going higher, no one is falling today. Dragon you are going hungry, nothing to feed off here!

It was a beautiful day for arguably the hardest IRONMAN® event on the planet. Jellyfish the size of Fiat cinquecento cars, rugby scrums in the sea almost every five minutes and especially around the buoys! During the swim I was punched and kicked in the head and stung by jellyfish, this Dragon was not going to go down without a fight!

THOUGHTS sent to COV TRI CLUB
14th September 2018

Cov Tri, for those about to become Avengers this weekend, WE SALUTE YOU! I just wanted to bring some thoughts from my IRONMAN® events journey this year and hope that it will inspire. I only really learned to front crawl with Cov Tri in January 2017, I had only run one marathon in 2000 at the tender age of 30 and couldn't really call myself a proper cyclist. Without much thought we chose to do our first IRONMAN® event in France 2017. In 2018 we have chalked up two: I offered to do IRONMAN® Norway with my cousin, in a bid to get him across the line, but the one I really wanted to see if I had the minerals for was IRONMAN® Wales. I am the living proof that ANYTHING IS POSSIBLE. Doing two full-distance events in a year is just plain bonkers

– truth be told, I did register for IRON-MAN® Wales at 2am after a few mojitos – nevertheless, if you want this, you have got this. There is nothing special about *me, I have no svelte-like frame, long legs or indeed lots of time to train for these events, but once you get that the race is 80 per cent mental you are already there. I wish you the very best in your own quest and hope that this email encourages you to press a register button and get your first, your next, your best IRONMAN® event booked up and smashed. YOUR Anything is POSSIBLE. TRI WELL! Rocky.*

Seeing my cousin, wife and Mum throughout the day gave me a great boost. They darted in and out of roads and crowds to strategically get to a vantage point and spur me on. I loved it. They shared that they loved it too, they had some giggles together in between their work as best crowd supporters of 2018! The enduring memory of this day is nearing the famous red carpet finishing tunnel, some 16 hours after the race start, and my Mum is leaning over the barrier saying, "Go on Rocky!" willing me on, full of pride (and relief too!). Well, I thought she was going to high-five me, but no, she was so elated that I was about to finish this gruelling race, and so swept up by the emotion, that she gripped my hand in both of hers, bringing me to a complete stop near the famous finish line, whiplash! Hilarious! I gave her a kiss and said, "I'm going to need my hand back to finish." Little did we know that a year later I would be the one holding her hand, trying to hold her back from a very different finishing line.

EXERCISE TIME:
CULTIVATING GRATITUDE

Keep a gratitude journal for 30 days. Write three things, just three each day, that you are grateful for. It begins simply, "Thank you for ...."

This could be for your daily challenges, for the gifts you recognise, or for the simple things. You choose and if you get stuck on thinking up three, you need to think again buddy – we have so much to give thanks for, see better!

THE R.O.C.K.Y ROAD
FOR CHURCHILL

Rise – It is often at our darkest times that it is demanded we rise. We are called, this was the way with Churchill.

Obstacles – Ironically for someone with a speech impediment, he is renowned as one of the greatest speakers of all time. He never saw the impediment as an obstacle, for him it was never bigger than the need to speak, to communicate his views, to save the world. Prior to becoming Prime Minister, in the other offices he held he had made serious misjudgements, got it wrong and was widely disliked, even by his own party. But the country needed Churchill in its Darkest Hour.

Choices – After Gallipoli, Churchill could have folded, he could have kowtowed to those in his party who were seeking peace with Nazi Germany, but after visiting Germany in the '30s he knew the Nazi machine, had picked up early on the anti-Semitism and knew that Hitler would not be pacified. You couldn't reason with such a warped view of the world and Churchill knew that only war could resolve this, and so he was brought in to be our wartime leader to protect our freedoms. He chose to stand, in spite of the odds, even when the Nazis were on the coast of France, eyeing the English Coast believing the fight was over. However, it was Churchill who said, "We shall fight them on the beaches!"

Kaizen – Churchill, like Ali, knew that he was destined for the world stage. He worked on his speeches until they were wordperfect. It was the war that called him to step up for his "finest moment." We needed a wartime leader, someone who had served in conflict and someone whose mettle had been tested, but who was strong enough to take a stand.

You – What are your challenges currently? How are you coping with them? Are you the best one to take them on, should you call in your own Churchill to give you that advantage, or do you need to morph into that Churchillian character: steadfast, encouraging, determined? If you have that in you then use it. Lord knows, just like in his day, you too will have many opponents, some who are actually supposed to be on your own team. Consider who your ally is in this challenge and as Shakespeare would tell you, "Cling to them with hoops of steel." Don't let anyone else distract you from your purpose; work with your allies to get the job done.

. . . .

MUSEUM OF MOMENTUM TOUR

Back with our Muse now and the latest board member of your mind sits there, pondering you. You have come to this book for something and now you are in your reverie, thinking about a challenge – you hear these words: "Never give in. Never give in, never, never, never" (Winston Churchill, 29th October 1941).

When challenges come, you decide to accept one or throw yourself into one, know your convictions and then you have something to draw on when the going gets tough. You can rise above natural talent and even natural drawbacks when you are acting for a noble cause and you believe in it. Overcoming that challenge is more attainable by focusing on what you will do and what action you are prepared to take. Be a bulldog, stand there on that beach, defiant, and make sure you gather those who will be by your shoulder, willing you through the challenges that you face or will face around you. Let people help, they want to. Churchill did not win the Second World War but what he did, and should be forever celebrated for, is take on the challenge with "the us," willed us through and made us believe we could win.

CHAPTER VII:
MINDSET

BILLIE JEAN KING

. . . .

"Reputation is what others think about you.
What's far more important is character,
because that is what you think about yourself."

Billie Jean King

Mindset: noun. **a set of attitudes or fixed ideas that somebody** *has and that are often difficult to change synonym mentality.*

An 11 year old Billie Jean proclaimed to herself that she was going to be the number one tennis player in the world, having only recently taken up the sport. What possessed her to think this way? Was she proving something to herself? Her parents? The world? In fact it would be a year later that the then 12 year old Billie Jean was looking around the tennis courts asking herself where is everyone?

What is great about Billie Jean is how she thought her way to number one and whilst on that epic journey, she looked around and saw the white tennis shirts, the white shorts, the white tennis shoes, the white players and just knew it had to change. She used her position to bring about change and she is still at it to this day. "It was all white," as she recalls[31]. Realising her privileged position, she made another proclamation: to fight for equal rights. The evidence is well documented that she did the first and when her tennis career ended she continued to fight.

If we look back to Chapter 1, to the Hero's Journey outlined by Campbell, you can see her path, how she forged it to become

---

[31] Brian Frank, (2021), 'Billie Jean King Had The Epiphany At 12: Tennis Is A Platform For Social Change', *LA List,* 20 August, available at: laist.com/news/arts-and-entertainment/billie-jean-king-had-the-epiphany-on-a-at-12-tennis-is-a-platform-for-social-change

more than a world number one. She became a crusader, the elixir that she brought/brings is that of equality, but she had to be world number one first to find that voice, that banner, and begin the crusade.

She paved the way for equal pay in her sport, but also became the trailblazer of what is possible in a world where women are marginalised. Not satisfied with her voice making change in this area, she becomes a major force within the LGBT community after coming out herself. She is an advocate of change, equality and possibility.

So, what causes a 12-year-old, who only recently bought a racquet with money that she had earned through doing chores, to say I am going to be number one in the world? That is vision, it takes drive, it takes purpose. It took her only 15 years to become the world number one. What would your 12-year-old self be saying that they wanted to be number one at? I wonder... And what about now? If you could be number one what would it be at? If you are number one in your field, learn from Billie Jean. When you get there the next job begins and that means pulling other people up.

ROCKY FILENAME

BJK
BILLIE JEAN KING

1

OCCUPATION	Athlete, Tennis Player (Well... 12-time Grand Slam winner)
MADE THEIR ENTRANCE	22nd November 1943, Long Beach, California
EDUCATION	California State University, Los Angeles, (1961-1964)
AKA	Billie Jean Moffitt BJK
ACHIEVEMENTS (SOME OF..)	1961 Became the youngest pair to win the Wimbledon women's doubles title with Karen Hantze Susman 1966 Wins Wimbledon 1971 First female athlete to top $100,000 in prize money in a single year 1973 Created Women's Tennis Association (WTA), using her position to threaten a boycott of the US Open because of pay inequality. Because of her actions this was to be the first to offer equal prize money. 20th September 1973 The Battle of the Sexes vs Bobby Riggs – not just a tennis match but one with high stakes for the women's movement if BJK lost

ACHIEVEMENTS (SOME OF..) CONTINUED	1975 wins Wimbledon again and announces retirement from the singles arena but remained formidable in doubles, winning Wimbledon 1979 and US Open 1980. BJK hung up her tennis shoes in 1990. Her trophy chest includes 39 major singles, doubles and mixed-doubles championships. New York even named their tennis venue after her in 2006.

Another first for BJK is that she was the first female athlete to admit openly her homosexuality. In doing so, she lost all her sports endorsements and her husband, but she had to answer the call of who she was. Many years later she said, "I didn't get comfortable in my own skin until I was 51 about being gay."[32]

The tennis court was a place where Billie Jean could hold court; initially this was about realising her potential and then it was about using the court to highlight how unfairly the world of sport treated the different genders – she stood for justice. Emboldened by finding her voice for equality, she then embraced her own sexuality and broke the mould by coming out, earning yet another medal in the process – that of The Presidential Medal of Freedom 2009 for being "An agent of change." This is the highest honour a civilian can earn in the US, President Obama went on to say: "They remind us that we each have it within

[32] (2013), 'Billie Jean King talks coming out', Associated Press, 7 August, available at: www.espn.co.uk/tennis/story/_/id/9545526/ billie-jean-king-discusses-coming-pbs-show

our powers to fulfill dreams, to advance the dreams of others and to remake the world for our children."

On our point of mindset, using tennis and childhood dreams, we must mention Richard Williams. Father to Venus and Serena Williams (tennis megastars like Billie Jean) he was born around the same time as Billie Jean but he decided that his daughters, his black daughters, in the ever so white world that Billie Jean had noticed, would be world-class tennis players. What is astounding about his decision, and about their journey, is that he would coach them, even though he was not a tennis player himself. He had a few lessons from "Old Whiskey," which was enough to start him off, and then coached the girls himself, who of course, became all that he had dreamed for them – mindset folks. It is real, "See it, start it..." Having that determined mind-set, a horizon or fixed point you are travelling too, makes your days rewarding, giving you purpose and direction.

EXERCISE TIME: REACH HIGH

Take your right hand and put it in the air as high as you can. Is that really as high as it can go? Do it again – right hand in the air as high as it will go. Are you stretching to your last sinew? Are you on your tiptoes? Are you standing on your chair? If you could reach higher than you did the first time, then why didn't you reach that high the first time? To all second chancers or those looking for their third act even, let us Rock!

When you have achieved as much as Billie Jean that horizon becomes much bigger; it moves from self to culture: "Every Generation has the chance to make it better," (BJK)[33]. When our journey becomes about more than us, when it stops being about me being number one to us being liberated, it becomes a movement. We become bigger than the sum of our parts; we make more number ones; we grow and develop those around us, the next generation, and from our trials and tribulations make the world a better place, a place full of potential and equality.

. . . .

iROCKY

As an 11 year old I felt safe, cared for and didn't want for anything. I had no dreams of being number one at anything. Where does that come from, that need to be world renowned? Is it that Billie Jean, like Ali, knew, felt or just had the hunger to be the greatest? Desire or just wanting the world to recognise their gifts? With Ali he had found his trade and was working on it – but the 11 year old Billie Jean played twice and then

---

[33] TEDWomen, (2015), *This tennis icon paved the way for women in sports*, May, available at: www.ted.com/talks/ billie_jean_king_this_tennis_icon_paved_the_way_for_women_in_sports

made her announcement. I ask you again, if you could be the world's number one at anything, what would it be? And what if it was as simple as just deciding, or just declaring it to the world? I dare you to do it – what have you got to lose?

. . . .

THE PILGRIMS CHALLENGE (MY B RACE FOR MARATHON DES SABLES)

2ND-3RD FEBRUARY 2019 – 66 MILES

This was my first official Ultra run – I am not counting the Caledonian Challenge (54 miles in 24 hours 2009) – as we walked all of it and moreover my focus was not on the 54 miles, it was just a day out with my mates. This was a very different gravy. I was alone, carrying a backpack and running poles, and had snow to contend with. There was no crew cooking us up a good bowl of pasta this time! It was me against me, or rather that universal truth, it is you against you. Backpack – check, trail shoes – check, poles – check! The pack of runners quickly thinned as the proper runners took flight. Keen to keep something in the basement I trotted on and as such got a wee bit lost with some of the other wannabe first time Pilgrim Runners. We found our way though (adding to the already massive mileage) and as the day progressed, I can't say I started "reeling them in" but I did get to see other folk as we chalked the miles up. It was definitely character building, especially when at the last checkpoint, one of the marshalls came up to me and asked if

I could run with a lass whose confidence had gone a bit. (Are you seeing a theme here? Why me? Well, because that is why I am here – to take people with me. That is my philosophy and you know when you commit to your own philosophy you WILL see the theme emerge). It was late and dark and it had been a long day, only three miles to go with 30 miles chalked up. Three miles might not sound a lot, but at that time of the day, in the dark and with the mileage you have already run now sitting in your legs, it is. This lass and I set off and she was very grateful. She had been waiting at the checkpoint for some time, she told me that she tried to do this last year, but hadn't been able to finish and I told her she would finish tonight. Through the dark, we started our final grind (well for this day anyway – tomorrow, after a sleep at the school hall we then had to do it all again and run back to the start!). She told me her name was Viv and she was, wait for it... 72. Yes, you read that right. She was so grateful to me, BUT I was the grateful one, not least of which I can only hope that at that age I have energy to sign up for similar events and then have the energy and determination to complete them. Her head had gone, so I shared my best Tommy Cooper jokes and we talked about our favourite music, all to get her out of that defeatist mindset. Then I asked what drives her? She said, "I have been to three funerals this year, and they were all younger than me." You see that sense of Memento mori pervades; it was death and loss that drove her to live. I loved spending that time with her. As we sat peeling off our muddy boots she thanked me once again and said she had decided to do day two as well – what a woman! One of the best ambassadors I have met for grow-ing old with attitude – a 'rager' as I would say with a nod to

Dylan Thomas, "Do not go gentle into that good night, rage, rage against the dying of the light."[34]

Viv was my very own Billie Jean that day. Born around the same time and still pushing back boundaries and letting age be just the number that it is and not a condemned sentence. You can do anything you want when you are 11 or even 60 years on from that – these women still are, what is holding you back? We are all pilgrims, all of us. Some causes are just that strong that they keep us moving, keep making us take that pilgrimage. Do you have that cause, that something that moves the spirit in you, or like your dreams is it buried? Now is the time to find it, there is help out there. Start the journey, get a coach (fitness or life or business); do not wait at a checkpoint, buddy up and move forward. You never know, it might be you who will be needed and may well be you who inspires those around you, even when you thought you were the one needing that push, that inspiration

. . . .

[34] Dylan Thomas, (1952), 'Do Not Go Gentle Into That Good Night' from *The Poems of Dylan Thomas*, New Directions

THE R.O.C.K.Y ROAD
FOR BILLIE JEAN KING

Rise – She decided at 11 years old that she was going to be a tennis world number one. 11 years old!

Obstacles – She fought off and on the court for equality, her coming out was met with a hard media response.

Choices – She chose to take on the establishment, men (battle of the sexes) and strive for equality. She is still striving, "we're not there yet."

Kaizen – From it's all about me, "I will be number one...", she moved on and up to: it is all about us, "That's the way I want the world to look: men and women working together, championing each other, helping each other, promoting each other — we're all in this world together," (BJK)[35] and arguably she has helped more people and continues to help them with this shift of mindset.

You – Leading us nicely to the question, are you still in an, "It's all about me" mindset? Or are you consciously working with and helping others with their battles, their struggles**?**

. . . .

[35] Paul Gittings, (2013), 'Pioneer Billie Jean King championed equality in women's tennis', CNN, 19 November, available at: h edition.cnn.com/2013/08/20/sport/tennis/tennis-billie-jean-king-wta-equality/index.html

MUSEUM OF MOMENTUM TOUR

Another Hall of Famer fills a place at the table – you decide if it is the child Billie Jean who just decided to be world number one, with that innate childlike naivety that we all had back in the day and that we still need sometimes when the task ahead looks impossible or our aging addled brains just say, "No" to the task. Or whether you have that vibrant 70 year old Billie Jean spirit by your side, saying, "No" to the "No" and still continuing her crusading; standing up, being visible, still working tirelessly for others, for equality and for what's right. She is famous for the battle of the sexes tennis match and being one of the best tennis players ever, but she, like Ali, broke out of her respective arena and had a voice. Billie Jean says, "The most important words that have helped me in life, when things have gone right or when things have gone wrong, are 'accept responsibility'."[36]

Right or wrong it is on us and when she saw something wrong she put the armour on and went on her crusade, at great personal cost and risk. Her mindset is a thing of beauty, crafted from her conviction and dedication. Even when she put the racquet down, she had a clear sense of fairness and used her time on the court to keep making the changes. As with Viv, she went Ultra to not be put in a box – both physically and mentally. Age does not define you, your actions do. Act well!

[36] Billie Jean King, (2000), *Amherst Commencement Address*, 21 May, University of Massachusetts, Amherst

CHAPTER VIII:
SUFFERING

JANE TOMLINSON

. . . .

"I am a mother, a sister, a daughter, a wife. And I happen to be a cancer sufferer. Why do I even have to be a sufferer? And what's brave about having cancer? Living with cancer isn't courageous. You make the choices you can in difficult circumstances."

Jane Tomlinson[37]

[37] Riazat Butt, (2006), 'What's brave about having cancer?', *The Guardian*, 29 June, available at: www.theguardian.com/lifeandstyle/2006/jun/29/healthandwellbeing.health

Suffering: *pain that is caused by injury, illness*, *loss, etc. : physical, mental, or emotional pain. : feelings of pain.*

. . . .

"Now let me tell you something you already know – life ain't all sunshine and rainbows..." (Rocky Balboa)

It was in August 2000 that Jane and her family received the devastating news that the cancer was back, and this time it was incurable. She was given six months to live. Rather than just making sure her affairs were in order, she went further, oh so much further. The athlete Jane Tomlinson was forged in the flames of chemo fighting cancer cells raging through her body. Jane signed up for the 2002 London Marathon – she was given six months and she signed up for an event way past that deadline – this was a woman who thought differently, fought differently and did so as she believed, we all have it in us to do so.

Jane was the first cancer patient to go the distance and complete an IRONMAN® full-distance triathlon (2.4-mile swim, 112-mile bike and 26-mile run). Her body was knocked about by the chemo, so much so that her heart was only at 60 per cent capacity. The cancer treatments were having a real impact and legend has it that only the week before the race she could hardly walk. As the sun came up on the morning of the 6th, there she stood though, ready to take it on and settle a score. Incredible!

June 2006 and Jane was on a 4,200 mile ride across America – San Francisco to New York, over 10 weeks with only 10 rest days scheduled in. Jane's health, by all accounts, had deteriorated badly at this point but she still was in the saddle for over 10 hours a day. She didn't think about her pain though as she was on a mission, a mission of her own design and that was to lead from way out in front, demonstrating by every push of the pedal that cancer does not define you. You are bigger than it and even though you have heard those words that no one wants to hear, you (borrowing once again from Dylan Thomas) "Do not go gentle into that good night."[38] Jane's own ethos was: "Death doesn't arrive with the prognosis." She started to dream big and take on challenges that healthy folk would think twice about. She decided to make a difference with the time she had left. This was not a woman to just crawl into her shell and die, no, she raised funds in excess of £1.8 million to support others. So what happened? Jane made a choice – when the obstacle of cancer shows up, we all have a choice.

"What I want to say to people is, yes, it is awful, but hey, you can still have a good time. What I'm doing is showing people you can still have a life even when you're living with a terminal illness." Jane Tomlinson[39]

[38] Dylan Thomas, (1952), 'Do Not Go Gentle Into That Good Night' from The Poems of Dylan Thomas, New Directions
[39] Jill Foster, (2007), 'Jane Tomlinson: An inspiration to the end', The Daily Mail, 5 September, available at: www.dailymail.co.uk/news/article-479984/Jane-Tomlinson-An-inspiration-end.html

I had, of course, heard of Jane Tomlinson but it was mostly about her being a London Marathon icon. When a friend gave me her book, *You Can't Take It With You* (Jane & Mike Tomlinson 2007), I knew how it ended so I was in no rush to read it. It was some five years later, whilst looking for inspiration to take on the IRONMAN® Nice (France) challenge, that I inexplicably picked the book off the shelf and started to read about this incredible woman. I had no idea of what she did and how she pushed back a six months prognosis to six-plus years, and I also didn't know that she took on the IRONMAN® Nice challenge. It was with goosebumps that I read about her signing up and getting to the start line, battling against the strong sea swim, only for her to be unceremoniously stripped of her race number at transition. As she missed the bike cut off time by minutes and her race was over, she was unable to get to the marathon. I still recall that sense of outrage – of course the volunteer didn't know that this was a woman battling against cancer, she wasn't just rocking up to chalk up an IRONMAN® race, this was her legacy, this could be her last chance, there may never be another opportunity. It was then and there that I decided that I would take Jane Tomlinson across the line in France. I scanned the cover of the book, laminated it and said you're coming with me Jane. This was a wrong that had to be righted.

As an aside: Run For All Leeds 10K is part of Jane's legacy, the fundraising for charity goes on and on. The Jane Tomlinson Appeal is still going strong, helping children and those suffering from cancer to have a better life.

THE HUMAN SPIRIT

Dr Viktor E. Frankl wrote *Man's Search for Meaning*[40]. This is a very important book that you must read; it gets referenced often but when he allows you to enter the world he survived and shares what he learnt through his suffering and that of others, we see, we feel, we learn through his suffering. I'm sharing his voice below; he was a notable psychiatrist before his imprisonment at the hands of the Nazis, even though he was not going to publish his work initially, he felt duty bound. Apart from a terminally ill patient, has anyone seen as much suffering as Dr Frankl?

He tells us: "Everything can be taken from a man but one thing: the last of human freedoms – to choose one's attitude in any given set of circumstances, to choose one's own way."

"Between stimulus and response there is a space. In that space is our power to choose our response. In our response lies our growth and our freedom."

"Everyone has his own specific vocation or mission in life; everyone must carry out a concrete assignment that demands fulfillment. Therein he cannot be replaced, nor can his life be repeated, thus, everyone's task is unique as his specific opportunity to implement it."

---

[40] Viktor E. Frankl, (2004), *Man's Search for Meaning: The classic tribute to hope from the Holocaust,* Rider

And on that note here is our next champion, Jane Tomlinson. Here is a woman who chose her attitude, her response, her mission: (Go Jane!)

ROCKY FILENAME JANE TOMLINSON Jane Tomlinson	
OCCUPATION	Radiographer, wife, Mum & total inspiration
MADE THEIR ENTRANCE	21st February 1964, Wakefield, UK
EDUCATION	Sheffield Hallam University
ORIGINALLY	Jane Emily Goward
AKA	Dame Jane Emily Tomlinson, CBE
ACHIEVEMENTS (SOME OF..)	An MBE, and subsequently, a CBE by the Queen The helen róllason award at the bbc sports personality of the year awards in 2002 Twice recognised at the sportswoman of the year awards A Great Briton award Voted the most inspirational woman in Britain in 2003 A pride of britain award in 2005 Author – The Luxury of Time and You Can't Take It With You

iROCKY

When I embarked on getting this book out of my head and into print, I never thought that part of the endurance events I had taken part in were to help in the fight with El Cancer. My Mum was diagnosed with bad cancer in September 2019, I say bad cancer, but is there any other kind? This one, however, had boots on – not only did she have bladder cancer but it had become metastatic and was now in two other organs. Her prognosis was not great: six months without treatment and perhaps 12 months with treatment. Now, if you have ever been in one of "those" meetings, time does seem to stand still and for a moment you are all alone; the stuff that once mattered immediately doesn't. This next part is not about cancer, it's about spirit. It's not about pain but how my Mum decided to "live" and not be her condition.

Chemotherapy attacks cancer, but it also attacks everything else, including the healthy blood cells. Mum's "dose" was receiving three cycles (a cycle was two sessions, one of which was long, circa eight hours, and the other short, circa two hours). It has been said that when someone is diagnosed with El Cancer (and I am borrowing this from Deadpool as you have to respect it, but you cannot fear it), the whole family gets cancer. What was once taken for granted and part of the routine, has to change. Perhaps as an only child or just because I saw a healthy, life-loving lady coming to terms with the news, I decided I would accompany her on all treatments, to be her cornerman on her biggest fight.

The first thing that struck me on entering the chemo annexe was a picture of my Tri Club – Coventry Triathletes, The Spots! – the banner was encouraging everyone to run 5K, a defiant act against cancer. I had to smile seeing them pose for the picture in their 'spots', the stand out Cov Tri colours. I also said thanks, as I didn't feel so alone now. It was good to see them on that poster and made what came next easier.

We walked into the treatment suite, the nurses were surrounded by a lot of sick people and their "grieving" relatives and I consciously say that, as something has died, something has changed. There is a new normal and it is so very different from what your world once was. That is not defeatist – in fact quite the opposite – the patients there, who are hooked up to various fluids, chemo, blood, clinical trial drugs, are sitting there undefeated. Like Ali, standing tall holding that Olympic Torch, as if to say, "I am still here." They are fighting their best fight, being their strongest self for the family that are on this "journey" with them. Who knows what they each have going on inside of them, not just with their diagnosis, but the bad medicine they are having to take to survive it. That first day, above all the others that came after, I saw SPIRIT, human spirit, raw, larger than the sum of all our parts. It could have been that I was walking in there, shoulder to shoulder with one of the strongest women I have ever known and her strength was infectious.

This spirit though was not just palpable in the sick, the nurses were just being themselves, and being totally caring for patients and in turn being their cornerman/woman alike. You are born with that, you cannot teach that. They know what is going on in everyone's minds, how no one wants to be there, but the alternative is not an option. While we are there on their watch, they are with us, and this is their world, week in, week out. I saw no one feeling sorry for themselves, although I am sure those moments come and when they do they are "inward." They are on a mission and they get on with it. Ironically when faced with so much death, you see life.

There were people in there who didn't know if this was their last Christmas, but for as long as they could, they would continue to be their strongest self, keep turning up and keep taking the bad medicine. I am including this section in the book because, as the man says, "The World ain't all sunshine and rainbows..." and you were warned that this chapter was called suffering. Perhaps the hardest chapter, but suffer we must, endure we must. I have to say, the miles and the endurance that I had chalked up to date was nothing and still is nothing compared to sitting next to my Ma, as she endured in the chair in an open ward surrounded by strangers. We picked our spot, Mum suited up for her fight, just her versus her opponent in the other corner, El Cancer. I took care of everything else so she could focus on her task but you can't help but feel useless, you just want them to get better. She knew she was never alone and hopefully this helped to buy her some time.

I will take this opportunity to apologise here to my wife and kids, and my clients as I focused at this time on my Mum. After all, all she had was me and I wanted to be there for her, as she had always been there for me. I had to rely on my staff more than I had previously had to; just as I was in my Mums's corner, I had great support in mine and so alongside the apology for perhaps not being as present as I would have liked, thank you for letting me be there 24/7 when I was needed most.

There are a number of references in this book to the Stoics – in a previous life my dear Mum must have been one. She never complained, there was never a, "woe is me"; she just got on with it, she endured the cancer without a negative word and she went through the chemo very stoically, "I've had a good life," she would often say. If my fate is to walk down that cancer path myself, I hope that I can be as strong, she really was incredible. That's not to say that it didn't knock it out of her. Some mornings when I came to collect her for her treatment, it took a lot of effort to walk from the car to our "chair" in the hospital and when I say effort, endurance races have nothing on it, it was as if there was no energy, no will and yet from somewhere she found it!

Could the girl from Rugby make it to the rugby though? The Six Nations was coming up and that famous annual battle the Calcutta Cup (Scotland vs England) this year was to be on 8th Feb 2020, at Murrayfield, Edinburgh. My little cousin decided to get tickets for us. The plan was for him, his wife and Mum and I to attend. That week would be something for Mum to look forward to. Mum was having a long day of chemo though and she was very weak at the time, getting her to Edinburgh looked impossible, that word again! Just getting her to the hospital for her treatment was a struggle. Only three times had she taken my arm, all the other times she was able to walk tall and as she would say, "put my shoulders back."

We continued to make the arrangements though and hoped and hoped. Little cousin had also managed to successfully bid for a weekend stay at Edinburgh Castle – The Governor's House – no less (NB Edinburgh Castle is not a hotel – it is essentially a barracks/officers' mess), so this is an absolute honour and dare I say a unique experience for a civilian. Anyway, even the lure of a stay at the castle seemed like fantasy looking at this woman who was struggling to walk from my car to her chair waiting for her at The Arden Centre for her next dose. The hospital knew that her bloods were low and were looking to book her in for a blood transfusion on the Friday 7th February. This of course was when we would have been travelling up, so we made it for the long day on the Tuesday and then, something happened...

The nurse who was caring for us was someone we hadn't met before (and we thought that we had met all the nurses and knew all their names and, the way Mum talks and listens to people, their life stories). This nurse asked us how we were doing and of course we told her that we were hoping to make it up to Scotland for the weekend, but with blood count low and Mum needing a transfusion, it was looking unlikely. This woman took it upon herself to get us booked in for the blood transfusion on the Thursday instead, to give us a chance to make Scotland and I am not sure whose blood she ordered but it was good stuff!

I turned up on Friday morning, not knowing what to expect, but there was Mum all packed and raring to go! Nothing short of a miracle, if you had seen her at any time that week, including just the day before, you would have thought as I did, no chance. We, of course, didn't take into consideration "the Penny Factor." Was it the blood? Was it that she knew that this may well be her last chance to get up to Scotland to see my cousin and his wife? Who knows but I am so grateful to that nurse, and my cousin, for making a great weekend come together. The drive up to Edinburgh was one of the best I have ever taken and I decided to go "the scenic route" via Moffatt – Mum loved it and it is days like this that I remember most now.

At Edinburgh Castle they were expecting us and we drove across the cobbled courtyard through a tunnel that looked like something from a James Bond film set – it had been hewn through the rock – and we parked up outside The Governor's House. I was still pinching myself (have you noticed how often I pinch myself? But I do, as this was nothing short of fantastic, reminding myself of where we came from and now there we were, staying at one of the highest seats of Scotland!).

Now, the weather didn't know that my Mum had had a rough week with her treatments – what showed up on the morning of the 8th for the famous Calcutta Cup was nothing short of a gale. Seeing my Mum walk from the car to the hospitality tent, through that unrelenting wind and rain, and only two days before she struggled to make it out of the car; was just inspirational. She was on her own Hero's Journey and no tempest would stop her. We made it up the many flights of stairs to our seats and even though the wind was bending the uprights, the four of us enjoyed huddling together and braving the game – respect to both teams for grinding through those conditions! We still had to make it back to the car after the game and back to the Castle for our last night as the temporary kings and queens of Scotland that we kidded ourselves into being.

We had breakfast together the following morning and then headed south. Due to the weather, getting out of Edinburgh was a lot harder than normal due to flooding and road closures, but we endured until, after about an hour's drive, we found ourselves on a very narrow road, through what was once a field (we could tell this as we could still see half of the fence posts). However, the whole place was under water and flowing at a pace. I drove to the water's edge and stopped, thinking if we got stuck, we would get proper stuck. Mum's chimp was out, "Turn back, turn back" or "No Michael, No" A four-wheel truck approached from the other side of 'the Tiber'. He must have read my mind, as he pulled alongside and told us that a car came through it earlier this morning, just to go slow and keep to the left. Geronimo (but with a small g) – off I went, with Mum holding on for dear life, and we made it. The rest of the journey I am happy to report, if only for my dear Mum, was uneventful.

That was our last trip north. Her chemo stopped in March. We lost Mum July 30th 2020, I was holding her hand.

Part of the journey has to be suffering, if this book was just about me bouncing from race to race, so what? You could do that yourself. No, I am sharing this most personal of journey's with you as it is how we react to the suffering, how we cope, that defines us. My Mum walked on through it, she suffered some, but endured more. Just like Jane, she wasn't about suffering and wearing a big badge that says I've got cancer – she fought quietly, but with all she had.

EXERCISE TIME: LEARN TO EMBRACE SUFFERING

When suffering comes, and it will come, don't be afraid, embrace it – that is the exercise for you, a slow burner perhaps but "embrace suffering." You might not need it now but mark those words, I promise you, they will help.

That's a heads up for you, remember those words. Embrace it, this is part of our life, it is part of your transformation, going to a different level. A butterfly can only become a butterfly and fly by enduring the caterpillar's existence, stuck by habit and gravity to the ground, on the horizontal plain, only dreaming of flight, anticipating metamorphosis. It emerges from the cocoon when the time is right – it might be days, it might be years but it has had to endure like you and I, to reach its potential to go vertical. The caterpillar may well want to remain as that eating machine, doubling its size on a regular basis, but try as it may to cling on to that life, change is a-coming, you can fight it if you wish or... EMBRACE it. Our world can change in a heartbeat. Look at Jane, she could have switched into victim mode and wasted her precious time but not a bit of it – she became that butterfly. I've got cancer, so I am going to run a marathon. I am having chemo, so I am going to cycle from Land's End to John O'Groats. If there was ever a woman who decided to let suffering take her to a higher level and help us all not fear it when it comes for us, it is Jane Tomlinson.

....

THE R.O.C.K.Y ROAD FOR JANE TOMLINSON

Rise – When given her diagnosis Jane decided to suit up and start running but it didn't end there – this woman took herself to a level hitherto unthought of.

Obstacles – Chemo, a poor prognosis and having a young family were all against her goals.

Choices – Jane had a choice and many opportunities when she was beaten to give up, but she never did. Her cycling challenge from John O'Groats to Land's End is just one of many examples. She still stopped to get her chemotherapy and then picked up from the last stop. Having nursed someone going through chemo and cancer treatments, the fact that she could lift herself time and time again is the stuff of legend.

Kaizen – Not satisfied with the London Marathon, Jane goes on and on and takes on and on – Ride across America – words actually fail me here. This woman was diagnosed with terminal cancer and she chooses to take this on, as well as these extreme challenges to rage against it.

You – Being a cancer patient did not define Jane. She is my ambassador for the Dylan Thomas lines, "Do not go gentle into that good night, rage, rage against the dying of the light." What are you defined by? And is it time to shake off the shackles and surprise yourself?

. . . .

MUSEUM OF MOMENTUM TOUR

What can Jane tell us? That we are capable of much more than we imagine? For sure. That we put limits on ourselves? Yes. Look at what she did for charity. What are you doing about charity? About making your time count? Jane thought she had six months and look at what she did. This is not a work of fiction. Check out what this lady accomplished through all the treatments and the weight of taking on cancer; she used her suffering, she worked through it, made it count and still to this day there are recipients of her work, for her daring greatly.

CHAPTER IX:

ACHIEVEMENT

THE ALL BLACKS

. . . .

"I was never good enough to play for the All Blacks. I'd give up everything I've done in coaching to play one game. And most people would say I'd be lucky."

Steven Hansen All Blacks Head Coach 2012-2019

Achievement: a thing that someone has done successfully, especially using their own effort and skill

....

THE MOST SUCCESSFUL TEAM ON THE PLANET

The All Blacks are synonymous with achievement. When it comes to rugby, how can such a small island/population have dominated a sport for over 100 years? (No need to send your postcards in – we will explore together).

They are the original and one and only! Interesting to note that they represent the country of New Zealand, but everyone knows them by their Rocky name, their nomme de guerre: the All Blacks. New Zealand sounds good, NZ sounds good, but that name, the All Blacks, sounds committed, all in, you know our colours. If you haven't decided your nomme de guerre yet, give it time, it will come. It will represent, it will resonate. The All Blacks of course aren't the only rugby team to dub themselves a playing name, there are the Pumas (Argentina), the Springboks (South Africa), we even have the British Lions! Summoning that animal spirit makes us bigger than the sum of our parts.

ROCKY FILENAME

THE ALL BLACKS
The New Zealand Rugby Team

OCCUPATION	Rugby Team
MADE THEIR ENTRANCE	1903, New Zealand
EDUCATION	New Zealand
AKA	Most successful Team of any sport, at any time New Zealand
ACHIEVEMENTS (SOME OF..)	Won Rugby World Cup 1987, 2011 and 2015 Hold a 77% winning record in test match rugby (bear in mind that some All Black coaches have had a 92% win rate) Only international team to have chalked up more wins than losses against EVERY other team Team of the year 10 times since the award began in 2001

There have been some outstanding players who have worn the All Blacks shirt, but the strength is very much TEAM. It is not always the best player who gets picked, but he who will wear the shirt with honour, have that sense of responsibility and pass the shirt on when his time comes with his head held high.

On All Black coaches, again there have been many of note, but to highlight individuals would take away what the All Blacks stand for. The team, its heritage and its legacy are bigger than the players and coaches. It is a movement, I would say phenomenon but that has a sense of freak occurrence; the All Blacks are like a fern tree growing in every international rugby pitch, unstoppable and one that keeps coming back year after year. No matter how you try to chop it down, it is relentless.

If you want to know more about how awesome the All Blacks are, read James Kerr's book *Legacy (15 Lessons in Leadership) What the All Blacks can Teach us about the Business of Life* – here you will see that it isn't only about rugby but much much more.

Sport inspires us as we witness those still on their journey, working on their craft, getting better, faster, stronger. They are looking at records and working to break them. This moves us because it reminds us that one day we used to focus on records, challenges, that thing that we believed made us, us. Do you still have your music inside you? Is that where you want it to stay? If not, what can you do about it? How can you let it out, like the genie in your bottle, what needs to happen to show us what you have got? Pick up the guitar again, that career you wanted, that great deed, that love of your life, do not let that road not taken never be taken, otherwise you risk looking back years hence with regret. Get your boots on and head down that road; you know where the current road you are on will take you, so instead head out and see what magic may happen, what have you got to lose? How much "loss" will you feel many years hence when you are filled with angst and a "coulda, shoulda, wanna" regret that you'll take to the grave. If you want to be that somebody you always wanted to be, take that potential and work it with the unrelentingness of Goggins, conviction of Ali and naivety of Billie Jean.

EXERCISE TIME:
YOUR ROCKY FILE

This book is for you and about you.
Over the next couple of pages I would like you to write down your achievements, what have you done (so far) with your time on planet Earth. Do not be shy, put down all of them, the small and the tall:

.

ROCKY FILE iROCKYU	
NAME	
OCCUPATION	
MADE MY ENTRANCE	
EDUCATION	
AKA	
ACHIEVEMENTS	

ACHIEVEMENTS TO DATE

BIGGEST ACHIEVEMENT (AGE)

....

....

....

....

....

....

OF ALL YOU HAVE DONE, WHY IS THIS YOUR BIGGEST?

....

....

....

....

....

....

PROUDEST ACHIEVEMENT (AGE)

....

....

....

....

....

....

WHY IS THIS YOUR PROUDEST?

....

....

....

....

....

....

....

WHICH OF YOUR ACHIEVEMENTS
HAS AFFECTED THE MOST PEOPLE?

....

....

....

....

....

....

WHICH ACHIEVEMENT IS NEXT
ON THE HORIZON FOR YOU?

....

....

....

....

....

....

HOW WILL YOU CAPTURE IT?/
HOW WILL YOU FEEL IF YOU DON'T?

....

....

....

....

....

....

WHAT WOULD YOUR TOP 3 TIPS
FOR A MEANINGFUL LIFE BE?

....

....

....

....

....

....

Write them down – whether you know it or not, there is a connection to the brain by holding the pen and putting your thoughts down on paper; plus, you should get them down and celebrate them!

ACHIEVEMENTS TO COME

MY BOLDEST PERSONAL ACHIEVEMENT

....

....

....

....

....

MY BIGGEST BUSINESS ACHIEVEMENT

....

....

....

....

FAMILY MEMBER BIGGEST ACHIEVEMENT

....

....

....

....

....

HOW WILL YOU FEEL WHEN THESE ARE CAPTURED?

....

....

....

....

....

....

Note how your answers would have been very different 10 years ago. Now think about how different they'll look in 10 years hence – what are you going to do with your time?

EXERCISE TIME: BUCKET LIST

Just as you did with your achievement list, write your bucket list here – this is for you. If you already have a bucket list and have done everything on there, write another one! The world is big, there are always wines you haven't tasted and dances you haven't danced. Be specific here though – Go to India, this isn't enough. When? See it, 'On my 60th, I want to see the sun come up whilst sitting on that bench by the Taj Mahal'. Who? Sense it – 'that beautiful tuscan dinner we had, alfresco, when we took the family on that Italian holiday in Florence, for our anniversary'. You get the idea – so what's burning? What's on the list?

....

....

....

....

....

....

....

....

Your full list will be a lot longer, if by any chance you are stuck and nothing is heading up the list, have you tried the Warren Buffet two lists method? First, write down 25 goals. Then from that list highlight the top five; it is those five that are your top priorities. The other 20 do not get touched until you have completed your top five. Try it – it's not as easy as it sounds, but it does help to focus your mind, time and intention.

iROCKY

Achievement looks different to each of us. For some it is money, for others status, for some it is being healthy, and there are those for whom just still being here is an achievement. I have added some of my achievements, but compared to not only the 12 case studies but many, many people's achievements they do not feature high on the scale of Everest climbs, world records, even IRONMAN® event times or number of races. It is about perspective and if you truly knew where I came from you would see it counts as achievement for me. This is what pressed me to write this book, so you could define what achievement looks like to you and go get it. Whilst on your quest though, here is another thought on achievement. During a trip to Vancouver a couple of years back, when we were helping out with a charity project over there, I did consider what my ledger currently stood at. For example, all the money and time and sacrifice given to charities, the man or woman on the street, those random acts of kindness, the fundraisers... If there was an accountancy statement when we shuffled off, how would I fair? Would I be seen as an achiever in this category? How would you fair, in this category of your life?

What would yours look like if you were to consider for one moment how much you have given to date? Be honest with yourself, the ledger is the ledger, you cannot fudge this. How much do you give each month by Direct Debit to the dog's home? Salvation Army? Cancer Research? If you see someone begging do you get them something to eat or drink, or give them money? Do you give your time, and this only counts if it is selfless not individual fulfilment by trying to further yourself, (like showing the snaps of you at the soup kitchen to try to convince the world what a great person you are). I am talking about doing your charity work silently, not looking for any props or dues. What does your ledger look like? If you are happy with your balance for your time here on planet Earth GREAT! If not, what are you going to do about it? The time is now – ACHIEVER, even OVERACHIEVER comes in many forms.

. . . .

THE R.O.C.K.Y ROAD FOR THE ALL BLACKS

Rise – Size matters? Tell that to New Zealand – take a look at the population and then tell me how they can be the most successful team in sporting history. That's a rhetorical question, the answer is they choose to be. The size of your ambition and legacy matters. If you have the passion and dedication they can rise, you can rise.

Obstacles – Individual ego, oftentimes they don't pick the best standout individual players, you have to be an All Black and you have to be a team player. The tyranny of greatness, you have to win and keep winning, you don't want to be the manager that destroys the reputation of the greatest team in history – just a little pressure on the shoulders.

Choices – How do you keep motivated when some teams have never beaten you over decades and decades? How do you show up, time and time again, and mark that groove even deeper in your team's greatness? What choice do you make when you "show up" – is it to mark that groove deeper, or are you just going through the motions? What do you do to be match fit for every game? What motivates you?

Kaizen – Even the All Blacks train; even the All Blacks have coaches and managers. What training do you do for yourself? If even the mighty All Blacks have a coach, what is so great about you that you don't? Do you want that enviable winning statistic, or just to get by? Worse still, do you not even try?

Who are you accountable to? If the answer is no-one, you will be getting away with murder. Own your development/growth and get someone to work alongside you to see it through – do not let yourself go.

You – Listen to the Haka from New Zealand, it is calling to you to a deep seated place in you, to rise to rise to rise: "IT IS MY TIME, IT IS MY MOMENT." It is a celebration of life, your life – if you can't celebrate your life, no else will. Dance your posture dance, your defiant dance, your style and keep dancing!

. . . .

MUSEUM OF MOMENTUM TOUR

The boardroom of our mind has suddenly got very crowded! Here we have a team, who for 100 years have developed a work ethic that is all about working hard, doing the simple things well, earning my place in the team and working hard to keep earning it. Here they stand, revered, formidable. They force us all to ask ourselves, what would I have to do to be an All Black, to be formidable in my field, to earn my shirt, my place? Do I work hard enough on my business? Hard enough on me? What would it take for me to be formidable? Find your Haka and achieve.

CHAPTER X:

INSPIRATION

CHRISSIE
WELLINGTON

. . . .

*"Hard work and an open mind – it's the only way to
realize the potential that is inside every one of us."*

Chrissie Wellington

Inspiration: the process that takes place when somebody sees or hears something that causes them to have exciting new ideas or makes them want to create something.

....

14th May 2016 was a big day for me; a client, now a friend, Remco offered to pick me up early that Saturday morning to go to the lake for my first open water swim, as a test drive for my 1.2-mile swim for the IRONMAN® 70.3 triathlon. We talked on the drive up and he introduced me to the legend Chrissie Wellington. "Of course you've heard all about Chrissie Wellington? A life without limits?" I hadn't and he told me about this inspirational woman who suffered from bulimia, worked through it and seemingly came from nowhere to become World Champion and took the world by storm. She sounded like a kindred spirit, fully embracing that IRONMAN® event strapline of, "Anything Is Possible ." I was starting to believe, in spite of my below average swim, bike, run skills. This lady put fuel on the fire of me wanting to take on the world of triathlon and see if I had the goods, to challenge myself to the core, to suffer, to come out the other end and in turn inspire others.

Chrissie Wellington is the original for me, the one who got me to believe in what was possible, moreover to question what was possible and oftentimes, whatever your goal, that's part of the challenge as we stop asking what is possible and just reside in that sanctuary we have built for ourselves in the comfort zone. But none of that for Chrissie: the first British triathlete World

Champion, the only one, male or female to become world champ within a year of turning pro. She retired, undefeated, after winning all of the 13 IRONMAN® full distance races she started. World record holder, IRONMAN® World Championship course record holder (2009-2013) – just awesome. She won the IRONMAN® World Championship consecutively (2007, 2008 and 2009). Due to illness, she couldn't make the start line in 2010, but in 2011 despite being involved in a crash whilst out on the bike shortly before the World Championship, she won again and became the 2011 World Champion.

She has been called many things, "remarkable" often comes up, "Superwoman Chrissie Wellington" even; meeting Chrissie, reading her books and seeing through YouTube what she has done and how she took the sport by storm moved me to action. She got me to question my limitations and strive.

I got her to sign my book and, after chatting to me for a short while, she wrote, "To Rocky, To all you have achieved and will achieve" – now that might not sound much to you, but doesn't it give you a clue to how Chrissie thinks? She wasn't just giving a talk and knocking out a few autographs – not this lady. She is forward driven and has a power. That "power" is not unique to her, we all have it in us, but her power is to lift and to inspire. I would like to think that I act in that way more often than not, with Chrissie though I feel that this is her modus operandi. If we could all strive for that, at least 80 per cent of time, just think what our world would look like. We have it in us – think about that for your next business meeting, your next parent/child chat. Think about those perceived limits and park them for a while, then lay down some tracks for that exciting onward journey for all YOU will achieve.

Nascent (unrealised potential) is a brilliant word, one of my favourite words, and Chrissie typifies it. Before she was dressed in the Hawaiian Lei and hailed as World Champion, her realising her unrealised potential truly began in 2004. Due to a commuter cycling accident, she went back to her swimming to aid her recovery – it was here where the genesis of the triathlete she was to become started to truly take form. She would be World Champion in five years! Sometimes we have to fall to get up and stand taller. Chrissie, it can be said, fell hard in 2004, but it was through this suffering through the fall that the future World Champion was starting to get sculpted, the traits rising to the surface and destiny got a little closer. I am not suggesting that you need to have an accident to find yourself, sometimes it can be the catalyst. But consider for a moment Chrissie had World Champion in her DNA – like an acorn, she had that mighty oak tree inside her, but like so many of us, all that potential, that greatness could have stayed within us, "gone to the grave with the music still in them."

If you take anything away from our time together, please look within yourself, dig deep and let that thing inside of you out. Now I get that you might be bored sick of the world of triathlon I have immersed you in, this is not about swimming, biking or running – those are just details, vehicles that have taken me down a path that I never thought I would travel and it has clearly brought something out in me. What is sleeping within you? What are you waiting for?

There are obstacles, we know this, but you have got to go through them, or around them, or over them or under them. Get this, Chrissie said of one of her early victories that she trained for just ten weeks whilst juggling her job. She overcame illnesses, (be it stomach bugs or shingles), to not only compete, but sometimes even break course records – yes, she broke a course record when she was sick; she even managed to break a course record whilst stranded, waiting to fix a flat tyre at Kona.

We all get inspiration from different avenues, but when Remco took me to my first lake swim in 2016 and told me about Chrissie, that was a real moment, the effects of which are still rippling out. I guess if you don't know about IRONMAN® event heritage, then Chrissie may not feature yet on your radar. 0.01 per cent of the population have completed an IRONMAN® triathlon, but it is not to the converted that I am preaching, it is to the uninitiated, the rest of humankind. You don't have to have done an IRONMAN®race to get what a force of nature Chrissie is (Veni, vidi, vici). She came, she saw, she conquered. And what a great champ. Humble, inspirational, living her totem, "A Life Without Limits."

ROCKY FILENAME

CHRISSIE WELLINGTON
Christine Wellington

OCCUPATION	Civil Servant (DEFRA), Athlete
MADE THEIR ENTRANCE	8th February 1977, Bury St Edmunds, UK
EDUCATION	Geography (BA) from Birmingham University, 1st Class (1998) MA (Distinction) Manchester University (2001)
AKA	Muppet
ACHIEVEMENTS	IRONMAN® World Champion 2007, 2008, 2009 & 2011 Author – A Life Without Limits, To The Finish Line MBE 2010 OBE 2016 Parkrun (Head of Participation/Health & Wellbeing) The clues about Chrissie were always there – in Nepal her friends would note that even if she was sick, she would still show up and do some crazy mileage on the bike. She entered the Coast to Coast 2006 (circa 250 km, swim, bike and kayak) – she came second but with no kayak experience. Later that year she won her age group with 10 weeks' training and working full time.

ACHIEVEMENTS CONTINUED	2008 despite being stranded for 10 minutes with a puncture (yep you've guessed it) she wins. 2009 she beats the IRONMAN (Kona) World Championship course record that was set in 1992 – her then-coach Dave Scott (another IRONMAN race Legend!) said that she did that with a hamstring injury! January 2nd 2010 bike spill – broke/fractured several bones after falling on black ice. Rather than taking that, "woe is me" attitude, she saw it as a forced time out and to take a good look at where she had come from and where life was taking her. Challenge Roth 2010 – Broke the course marathon record with new IRONMAN full distance world record time 8:19:13

IRONMAN® World Championships 2010 – She did not start (DNS) due to illness, but, get this, after recovering from pneumonia only six weeks later she goes to Arizona and sets a new world record! And this, despite doing the last couple of miles of the bike course on a flat tyre. To be awesome is one thing, but if that was just Chrissie's story, she wouldn't be featured here. Let me take you to 2011. She has made herself faster and stronger to retake her IRONMAN® World Champion crown, however she is involved in a bike crash in the September of that year, with the World Championship looming on 8th October. She has no broken bones, but severe road rash with all contact points (leg, hip, elbow) giving her excruciating pain and leaving her having to use crutches to get around. All she could do at that time was swim, but she had to be lifted in and out of the pool and could only do a couple of laps. She managed to get an infection in her leg too, requiring antibiotics. This is what champions are made of though! Fuelled with the disappointment of not being able to compete in 2010, Chrissie saw through the pain, infection and road rash and stood on the start line 8th October 2011 and yes she went on to victory, of course she did.

We, all of us, borrow from Shakespeare and just in case you didn't get enough in our earlier chapter, it has been said of her in retirement, no less, she "doth bestride the world of Ironman like a Colossus," (*Julius Caesar* Act I Scene II).

Chrissie Wellington used to write Kipling's '*If*' on her drinks bottle and revisit it for courage and inspiration. Here it is for you now. Kipling gives us some key ingredients on the way to live, taking it on: "Keeping your head... Trusting yourself... Don't deal in lies... If you can dream, and... Stoop and build 'em up, heart, nerve and sinew, Hold On!". Great stuff eh? Here it is in its full glory:

> *If*
> *If you can keep your head when all about you*
> *Are losing theirs and blaming it on you,*
> *If you can trust yourself when all men doubt you,*
> *But make allowance for their doubting too;*
> *If you can wait and not be tired by waiting,*
> *Or being lied about, don't deal in lies,*
> *Or being hated, don't give way to hating,*

And yet don't look too good, nor talk too wise:
If you can dream—and not make dreams your
master;
If you can think—and not make thoughts your aim;
If you can meet with Triumph and Disaster
And treat those two impostors just the same;
If you can bear to hear the truth you've spoken
Twisted by knaves to make a trap for fools,
Or watch the things you gave your life to, broken,
And stoop and build 'em up with worn-out tools:
If you can make one heap of all your winnings
And risk it on one turn of pitch-and-toss,
And lose, and start again at your beginnings
And never breathe a word about your loss;
If you can force your heart and nerve and sinew
To serve your turn long after they are gone,
And so hold on when there is nothing in you
Except the Will which says to them: 'Hold on!'
If you can talk with crowds and keep your virtue,
Or walk with Kings—nor lose the common touch,
If neither foes nor loving friends can hurt you,
If all men count with you, but none too much;
If you can fill the unforgiving minute
With sixty seconds' worth of distance run,
Yours is the Earth and everything that's in it,
And—which is more—you'll be a Man, my son!
If by Rudyard Kipling (1943)[41]

41 Kipling, Rudyard (1910). rewards and Fairies (First ed.). London: Macmillan

Anything in there for you? Every time I read it something resonates. It asks the question of us – what do we value? How do we represent? Moreover, WHAT do we represent? When life throws something at us, what have we got in our kit bag and when there is no kit bag how do we move on? How do we keep moving on?

....

iROCKY

So how did I get on in my UK Triathlon Ultimate half (70.3 miles) in June 2016? Armed with Chrissie's achievements, in spite of the accidents and challenges along the way, I told myself I could do this. Well I swam it with a painfully slow breaststroke, but my thinking was if I could only make the cut off time and get on to the bike I would be okay. I was the last man to get out of the lake, beating the cut off by only three minutes. I was elated by "surviving" the swim and still pinching myself for going the longest distance I had ever swum. On to the bike and the rest is history or, as you have read, the rest is future! Buoyed by Chrissie and now with an IRONMAN 70.3® event under my belt I went large, I went Ultra and if I can, you can. We just need to have the right voices in our ear, encouragement, not defeat, wings and not millstones.

Choose your sources and use the MUSEum as those voices will only lift you. Learn from them, let their determination, their being, all they can be, affect you and let the kernel that is inside of you start to take root and branch out, being all that you can be. We, all of us have that acorn inside of us – right now, even as you read this, it might be something in the world of sport, it might be your business idea, it might be that you are looking to be the best version of you and you know you have let some setbacks and the years get in the way. Now is the time. It is never too late to let that DNA, the very same you were born with, do what it was born to do, inside of you.

I am going to mention that M word again here – Magic. Here I am bringing in the Periodical cicada. It's an insect and members of their clan are called *Magicicada* (I'm not making this up – go check it out). They live for 13 or 17 years – scientists don't know why the creatures have decided to opt for a prime number, let us just say that it is their nature, their magic. What is amazing is that these creatures live underground and then have this irresistible urge to surface, and they emerge as one and fly. They wait, wingless, underground for years and years for the right temperature (around 65 fahrenheit/18 celsius) and when the soil is ready for their passage, they grow wings and so the cycle continues. Why 17 years? Some say that as they feed off the tree roots, they can feel the cycles pass; others say that they have a molecular clock, but why bring insects to our celebration of human achievement? Well it's because I want you to be good to yourself. I do not want you to write yourself off because you are 30, 40 or 50 years down the line and you haven't achieved, maybe you are as baffled as scientists over the cicada clock – maybe your cycle is every 20 years, 40 years; maybe your time is age 47?

You have greatness in you, don't let a sense of underachievement get in the way. Maybe it is just not your time yet, maybe you have to cook a little more, maybe you need an unforeseen event to channel you down a path, maybe the temperature needs to be right, you might just be in your wingless state but your time is a-coming. Believe, keep working on yourself and you will know when the time is right. And if you feel that time has passed you by or, your chimp is telling you you just aren't good enough, do your version of a 1.2-mile swim when you are a rubbish swimmer and see what you can learn about yourself. I'm not suggesting for a moment you sink or swim – I was never in danger of drowning, no, I'm not for a moment suggesting you put your life on the line. This is a matter of life and death though: living the life that you want, or letting it slowly die and pass away a bit more year after year, after year, after year. Perhaps it's this year? Perhaps next? You will have your year though; you will have your time in the sun just like our *Magicicada* here.

EXERCISE TIME: WHAT IF?

What if you saw yourself as Mr or Mrs INSPIRATION? If you were to be known as THE Inspirer – who would your audience be? What would your "thing" be? Pick someone, or even a group, if you are feeling bold, and do something today. If you are reading this in a log cabin away from the world, at the very least ask yourself, who are you inspired by, what moves the spirit in you? And make plans for how you can move that forward.

THE R.O.C.K.Y ROAD FOR CHRISSIE WELLINGTON

Rise – Here is a woman who rises from an eating disorder to take the triathlon world by storm in her first year as pro. A World record breaker!

Obstacles: Crashes, inexperience (winning the World Title within a year of turning professional).

Choices – Chrissie documents her relationship with Brett Sutton – she endured and became World Champ, coming from nowhere. She started at day one and worked her way to the top. Just watch her, taking on her fourth World Championship, showing the war wounds from her accident only a couple of weeks before, nothing was getting in her way.

Kaizen – Constantly working on herself, even in the low point of the aftermath of the crash. Even after her triathlon career, she continues to make sport accessible by being a ParkRun ambassador and is still passionate about her original work of working with developing countries. She keeps going.

You – Listen, it doesn't matter where you have been, what you have done, the good, the bad and the ugly. Day one for you can start today, if you want it – what is your passion? Pick your coach, work on yourself and your goal – go get it! When the tough times come, dig deep and remember Chrissie – cut, grazed, swollen and in excruciating pain – she stands on the line to tell the world, in spite of all the obstacles, "This is mine!"

....

MUSEUM OF MOMENTUM TOUR

At the tenth spot on the outside of our horseshoe-shaped table sits Chrissie Wellington. Passionate about development, an undefeated world champion in a sport she accidentally landed in and then ruled. Remember, to enter this building you just need to breathe and see it in your mind's eye – our boardroom is getting full and each place represents discovery, encourage-ment and a focus. Take a moment to visualise it, not so difficult in our world of Zoom meetings etc to see those screens filled with a face, a unique personality and someone that may add value to your life. Consider this when you take a moment to reflect on each chapter and the soul or souls attached to it.

The phoenix is part of the emblem for The R.O.C.K.Y Project and thinking about her grit in coming back after the crash, covered in road rash, we can see the phoenix in her. So, what can she add to our mix in our reverie, our Muse, our MUSEum of Momentum? I just hear her whispering, "If"... "If"... "If...". If you think you can win at ANYTHING you are halfway there. Chrissie advocates a life without limits. Try it, take the brakes off and see where it takes you. "If you can dream—and not make dreams your master" – dream big but don't just let that thing, whatever it is, just live only in your Muse as a dream. Take action, work at it, take it from a dream to a chapter in the book of your life.

CHAPTER XI:

LEGACY

MICHELANGELO

....

"Your gifts lie in the place where your values, passions and strengths meet. Discovering that place is the first step toward sculpting your masterpiece, Your Life."

Michelangelo

Legacy: something that somebody has done successfully and that has positive effects even after they retire or die.

....

A painter, viewed then and now as one of the best of his age, although he wanted to be regarded as a sculptor and an architect, of which much of his greatness has survived. His career lasted for more than 70 years but his legacy continues. He is seen as the archetypal "Renaissance Man." The brilliant Michelangelo crafted many masterpieces, including "David," the "Pieta" and the ceiling of the Sistine Chapel. He is the artist often called "the Divine One".

As a teen, Michelangelo was sent to live and study in the home of Lorenzo de' Medici – (how greatness attracts greatness?). The young sculptor went on to linger in Rome for the next several years, eventually winning a commission to carve the "Pieta", the work that first made his name as an artist.

What lessons have we learnt? Michelangelo, going to the forum, said he was "going to school." If a master such as he could still be learning what are we doing about our "going to school?" Or do we think we are done, that we are the finished article, that we have arrived – can it get no better than this? There is a lesson from Michelangelo here: we are never done, never full.

Let us stop the history lesson for a moment and consider: Did Michelangelo consider what his legacy was going to be? Did he consider that we would still be enjoying his creations and talking about the man 400 years after his death? Or did he just make wonderful works of art, one at a time?

ROCKY FILENAME

MICHELANGELO
Michelangelo Buonarroti

OCCUPATION	Artist, Sculptor & Architect
MADE THEIR ENTRANCE	6th March 1475, Caprese, Italy
TOOK THEIR LAST BOW	18th February 1564 Rome, Italy
EDUCATION	Apprentice
AKA	Michelangelo The Divine One
ACHIEVEMENTS (SOME OF..)	Sculptor La Pieta David Painter The Sistine Chapel and Last Judgement Architect St Peter's Basilica Dome Piazza del Campidoglio: Capitoline Hill Basilica of Santa Maria degli Angeli e Martiri: Piazza della Repubblica

THINKING OF YOUR LEGACY

I now ask you reader: What will your legacy be?

I have had the good fortune to have lived in Rome and visited the Vatican many times but it was a certain guide who made me look at a statue I thought I knew and see it in a different light. Read on and see if this resonates with you too. La Pieta (the pity) is a statue of Mary and Jesus. He is lying in the Virgin's arms, after his crucifixion. But did you ever look at Mary's face? Don't you think that she looks so young? Too young? This is the genius of Michelangelo; he is conveying, through marble (his vehicle of expression), that this is Mary, chaste and pure and therefore not prone to the effect of aging, which is why she looks so young.

Moreover it was put to me that this is not Mary post crucifixion, but shortly after she had given birth to Jesus, and this is the baby Jesus in her arms; but she sees what his destiny is to be and that is why she is so young in sculpture. Now, this is just a piece of stone right? This lump of rock is hundreds of years old, has survived two World Wars and a heinous vandalism attack. Still it lives on, still it inspires us and will continue to do so when we are gone. Why do I mention this? It is simple, what is your legacy? What is your message, the message that will outlive you? You don't need to be a near-mythical Italian sculptor with a divine gift, you can decide right now, for example if you want a hospital wing to be named after you; to create a shelter for the homeless; establish a trust fund for your children and your children's children – it is in your hands, just as the chisel and cloth was in Michelangelo's.

We cannot overlook that this book is our homage to the underdog, and one of Michelangelo's best works or most famous pieces is that of David. The archetypal underdog – the shepherd boy who was pitched in the life and death battle against the giant Goliath. The magic of Michelangelo though is he sculpts David as the giant in his work, giving him stature and gravitas. This is not an art lesson however – let us look at the David story, the underdog won. How did he win? Through faith. He BELIEVED he could. When many had lost hope, he stepped up, he believed. David, Michelangelo, you and I, we need to believe and as life chips away at us, we too must keep chipping away at that which is most dear, to craft it, to make it a lasting statue of that part of us, something that defines us. We have referred to it as your philosophy or your totem, nail your colours to it.

When we look at lifetimes or big projects, just think that as Rome wasn't built in a day neither was Michelangelo's ground breaking, world-changing David. He showed up with his tools, knowledge and expertise and just chipped away at the marble, day after day. He kept chipping away and finessing until he was satisfied that his David was as good as it could be. What more can we do? That goal/project of yours, that diet, that habit – just keep chipping away, do not expect to have that sudden shazam moment and you are that David you have had in your mind's eye. You need to chip away.

Can you think about that for a moment? Let's say you want to lose weight – stop buying junk food. Let's say you want to pass exams which seem insurmountable – make time and study for them (you have the same 168 hours in a week, remember). If it is hard to find study time, make a study timetable, block time out of your diary and allocate that time so that nothing can get in the way of it. If it is about getting fitter – instead of lunch at the deli, which is what you have always done, take your trainers and shorts and run! Commit your time/timetable to your fitness and chip away.

It was said that when Michelangelo was asked how he created something so lifelike with his David he replied, "I just took away all the marble that wasn't David." Genius alert! He probably said it incredulously, thinking what a stupid question to be asked. After all he saw David, it was his vision, it was the aim and focus of his life for two years, he saw it all day and probably went to his bed dreaming about it. But delving deeper, if you have a goal, anything that doesn't take you closer to it, by definition, takes you further away. We have to obsess, we have to see it, work towards it and in our actions and habits, chip away. Consider what the tools of your trade are. Are they people, tech or a commodity? You might even be the commodity, it might be your time, your experience – finessing how you apply your time will help create that masterpiece of you, visualise and act upon it. What are you waiting for?

. . . .

ALL THE WORLD'S A STAGE

Living by your totem – when you decide that you are on this Earth to help "stuff" happen (so be very clear about why you are around, be specific).

Back in my drama school days I was fortunate enough to take a play to Romania, in 1994. It was a great festival of theatre, a gathering of theatre companies from around the world and most memorable for me, one from Japan, another from the Netherlands, along with our hosts. Our contribution was well received and I got on well with some of the actors from the host nation's theatre company. It was a whirlwind and they had me on a friend's radio station and then off to their family home for a big family dinner; they really opened their hearts and home to us. It was all very full on. What I couldn't have prepared myself for, however, was several years later, when their theatre company was performing at the NIA (Birmingham) and I naturally went to support them and took them for one of our best British dishes: a curry in the home of Balti, Birming-ham. One of the actors asked me to help him defect! And so we tried to jump through hoops for this guy with the Home Office and, whilst he was waiting to see if his asylum was to be agreed, he stayed with me and my family. I have stopped asking, "Why me?" I just know that I am here to help, perhaps it is simply because I have decided this is so – hopefully this will be part of my legacy.

You know we really aren't kicking around on this green and pleasant land for long, if you get a sense that I am urging you urgently into action then it is because none of us know how much time we have left, but what we can control is what we do with our time. If you are in a situation where you feel you cannot control your time, well my friend, you need to make some changes and do it now because if you aren't controlling your time then someone will. This is your time on planet Earth – do not be a time slave to anyone. We all have to make much of our time – we are duty bound.

This next passage draws to your attention a soul whose time ran out and he ponders his last moments, his legacy. The following is a poem most have never come across. Written by a plotter, assassin, martyr or put simply a 23/24 year old man on the eve of his execution. Chidiock Tichborne was born into a Catholic family which became embroiled in the Babington Plot to assassinate Elizabeth I. It was written, during his final moments, from the Tower of London on the eve of his execution for treason, along with a letter to his wife.

My prime of youth is but a frost of cares,
My feast of joy is but a dish of pain,
My crop of corn is but a field of tares,
And all my good is but vain hope of gain;
The day is past, and yet I saw no sun,
And now I live, and now my life is done.
My tale was heard, and yet it was not told,
My fruit is fallen, and yet my leaves are green,
My youth is spent, and yet I am not old,
I saw the world, and yet I was not seen:
My thread_is cut, and yet it is not spun,

And now I live, and now my life is done.
I sought my death, and found it in my womb,
I looked for life, and saw it was a shade,
I trod the earth, and knew it was my tomb,
And now I die, and now I was but made;
The glass is full, and now the glass is run,
And now I live, and now my life is done.
Elegy (1586) Chidiock Tichborne

To think that during his final hours, with the scale of his crime meaning no chance of a reprieve, he captured his life with ink and parchment. A testimony that he was here. Albeit brief, albeit half lived, albeit done – he chose to write poetry and it is this that has outlived him, with me including it here, some 430 years after his passing. We do not take any position on his crime. We include his elegy as this is palpable. This demonstrates how one values time when the sand from the hourglass is running out. Listen to him and let his words make sure that you are not left unfulfilled, half lived. His message is echoed within this book to make much of time for us all, before it is too late.

EXERCISE TIME:
WRITE YOUR OWN ELEGY

Write your own elegy. What do you want them to say about you? About how you lived (they say the ancient Greeks measured a person by asking the question, "Did he live with passion?", what would your answer be to that? Moreover, what would others say of that question when you have shuffled off this mortal coil?) Who do you want to give the talk about you? Whatever you would like them to say about you, think about how you can make those things come true between now and then. Consider for a moment that by your daily actions you are writing that elegy. Every day you do this by how you affect those nearest to you and, perhaps more importantly, those not near to you personally BUT you help them anyway.

Appreciating that one day we will be dead helps some to live, the Stoics knew a couple of thousand years ago, have we forgotten something? To drive this point home I would like to bring in   Bronnie Ware, *The Top Five Regrets of the Dying: A Life Transformed by the Dearly Departing*[42]. Bronnie worked in palliative care for many years and was often the last person the terminally ill spoke to, almost a mother confessor figure,

---

[42] Bronnie Ware, (2012), *The Top Five Regrets of the Dying: A Life Transformed by the Dearly Departing*, Hay House

or perhaps just a friendly soul, who listened and gave them time. She noticed the main themes of these poor souls who were preparing for their last bow. The same themes came up again and again.

Let us see what we can learn and inform how we live from today until our last morning. These are the top five regrets – in ink before your very eyes, so that you can live your life and be sure that they aren't going to yours:

1. I WISH I'D HAD THE COURAGE TO LIVE A LIFE TRUE TO MYSELF, NOT THE LIFE OTHERS EXPECTED OF ME.

Shakespeare wrote some 400 years earlier in *Hamlet*, Act I, Scene III – Polonius' advice to his son Laertes "To thine ownself be true" – ancient wisdom indeed, if it was right then and right now with those who are dying and reflecting on their time. Heed the warning people!

2. I WISH I DIDN'T WORK SO HARD.

Not to be confused with being a hard worker, this regret was based on those putting work first, at the expense of family, relationships and health. Take this time to check in with where you currently sit on this one. Any changes or tweaks required on your priorities? Remember we have included this so that this will not be a regret of yours – the time is now to make any key note changes. Do not wait!

3. I WISH I'D HAD THE COURAGE
TO EXPRESS MY FEELINGS.

Okay this is a biggie – if you have spent a lifetime keeping it all in, how do you express yourself and open up? How do you break that habit? As with any habit, the answer is one day at a time. Today tell someone how you feel about them, tell someone how you feel about you, your life, your dreams – try it and see what happens.

4. I WISH I HAD STAYED IN TOUCH WITH MY FRIENDS.

Life gets in the way doesn't it? That school friend, uni friend, ex colleague, current colleague, distant relations – there are those whom you have burnt the candle at both ends with, you relished spending time with them, but then you went on to the next chapter or they did and those time were left behind. What we must do is invest today to create more memories, burning more candles together, so that in our old age, dotage or if we ever find ourselves in the presence of a palliative nurse like Bronnie, this won't be one that we'll be taking to the grave. No, we will be sharing the good times, telling our tales and adventures!

5. I WISH THAT I HAD LET MYSELF BE HAPPIER.

Life is a choice. It is YOUR life. Choose consciously, choose wisely, choose honestly. Choose happiness.

What will your legacy be? Were your dreams crushed, a natural talent wasted or like a treasure you have buried it, to keep it safe but not had the time, energy or guts to dig it up? Are you someone who can look at a piece of marble and see a 'David', life, someone who has the art in them to create? Or are you now just a critic, pointing out where someone got it wrong or where someone could do better? What is your contribution and what do you want it to be? Make your mind up as time is passing and soon you won't be able to influence what you are remembered for – you are done.

Until then, let us take up the chisel metaphor and create our Duomo, Sistine Chapel, Church, La Pieta on such a grand scale (and why not?) or on our own scale: raise £100,000 for charity, do a fun run for the local hospice, volunteer in the community and let my kids see so that they in time will give their time to help others, or be remembered for your random acts of kindness. Do not leave it too late, remember the message from the protagonist in Leo Tolstoy's *The Death of Ivan Ilych*: "What if my whole life has been wrong?" When we are lying there, taking our last breath, it is too late – you have between now and then to do something about it.

We have included our very own "David" here – David Goggins! As a living and breathing work of art, look at what he did! Like Michelangelo, he got rid of the stuff that didn't work. Start your work today and get rid of those things that you do that are not serving you well. Chip away! Chip away today!

. . . .

iROCKY

I have already told you about my mate Sharon and how we lost her in 2003. That year was truly an annus horribilis, as we also lost Jim who was only in his 20s – not even three decades to build his life's work. We mentioned his great smile and his unique way of cheering me on through my first London Marathon. A lovelier bloke you couldn't meet but his tale is he was driving, just going to get some food for the team following a volleyball tournament, when he was involved in a car accident. It was just another day, but for those who knew Jim actually it would change everything. How you look at life, question your faith, and ask what is it all about!

There will always be this infamous moment in time, where I can picture Jim at the wheel and the other driver, the villain of this piece and the thief of Jim, recklessly and mindlessly veering onto the wrong side of the road, causing a head-on collision. Sadly, that was the end of Jim's story.

I laboured over a letter to his parents, to convey what a beautiful soul Jim was. I wanted to get everything in and how this loss, above everything else that had ever happened in my life, was just so senseless, why? why? why? I had to get everything in, all the times we'd shared, including that even though he was in Australia on my wedding day, he sent a telegram to say that as I was getting married in a castle in Scotland, he was claiming 'Prima nocta' (That's a Mel Gibson's Braveheart movie reference for those who are scratching their heads. It is about the English lords having 'first night' with the newly married woman). Yes we smile, that was Jim, he just made people smile. The colour spectrum in my world lost a colour when we lost Jim. I wanted to pour everything in, all we got up to and how I felt about their son who was one of my best people, and how proud they should be of him. Perhaps it was my way of trying to deal with and to try and make sense of this senseless loss.

I laboured and I laboured on this letter. My wife knew how I felt about Jim, she could see me pouring myself into this. She, with a hand on my shoulder, leaned in and said, "Babe, you can't get Jim on a piece of paper." He was only on the planet for a short time, but it's true he couldn't be confined to my writings, he was and is bigger than that. He cannot be contained in a letter; he, like all of us, was beautiful and complicated, unique and never to be seen again.

We are a work of art, chiselled away by time – and here we are. The outrage that I feel about that fateful day will never go. It isn't just that this was the day Jim died, but everything that he could have done, all that he could have become died that day too. Please, now that you know Jim too, make your time count. Don't take it for granted, live with purpose.

Here we are talking about legacy like we have all the time in the world – for some this is not the case. If I have two friends who were ripped away from me, you must have had someone too. Don't let their story end, let knowing them affect you to live harder, fuller and with a greater sense of purpose. Man!

What would they give for another day? While we have the day ahead of us let us live it, if not for us, then them. Let them live on in you.

....

THE R.O.C.K.Y ROAD FOR MICHELANGELO

Rise – Truth be told, I don't have the faintest idea what his motivations were. He had a talent and seemed to push back against being a painter, yet arguably the Sistine Chapel is one of his enduring legacies. How he brought life from a stone with the tools of the age is a complete mystery to me. I can see why he was called divine though, as he seemed to give life, whether in marble, canvas, ceiling or Church. Perhaps it was the divine in him that meant he could never be a secret and fame would always find him.

Obstacles – Not wanting to paint when the world wanted him to paint, personality clashes with Popes, the tyranny of his youth when he did La Pieta for the Vatican.

Choices – As an artist, he took commissions. Some of these meant that he was compromised, some he hated, but he brought beauty with him to each and every project. That reminds us that we have a choice on how we react to our work – do we just knock something out or do we labour and give it our best shot? Can we bring a sense of beauty to what we do?

Kaizen – When in Rome, he would go to The Forum "to learn". He constantly worked on his craft, looking for inspiration. If someone as brilliant as Michelangelo kept working on his craft, who are we mere mortals to settle and tell ourselves we can't improve/finesse/perfect?

You – Where do you get your inspiration from, where are your go-to places? Ask yourself what are your best creations? If they are your kids, as many will answer, how are you helping them to become the best version of themselves? If it is your business, same question. If your answer is me: you are the best creation that you have worked on and you have laboured on for years and hopefully you are very happy with the work of art that is you. What are you doing to maintain that work of art that is you? Warts and all, what are you doing to work on you?

. . . .

MUSEUM OF MOMENTUM TOUR

Here we have a man who was working until the day he died; he poured his time and soul into creation. He is here in our MUSEum now working with you, on you. Like it or not, art is in all of us, from the way we dress to the way we write and how we construct/live our 24 hours. We each have our studies, offices and/or workplace where we do "our thing," so what are you doing about being the best version of you, chipping away and taking out the parts that are not you, that don't belong? All the while finessing the parts of you that you want to highlight and bring out of the shadows. Keep working on you as Michelangelo worked away on that shepherd boy, the boy who would be King. Keep working is what he is telling you, keep working, keep perfecting till the day you die.

CHAPTER XII:
ALCHEMY

MARIE CURIE

. . . .

"A scientist in his laboratory is not a mere technician,
he is also a child confronting natural phenomena that
impress him, as though they were fairy tales."

Marie Curie

Alchemy: *a mysterious power or magic that can change things*

....

Her chapter is entitled Alchemy as she took the invisible (rays, I grant you) and made an impact on the physical. She rests today at the Pantheon, but her rays continue to shine and give hope and care today.

We have talked about magic in this book – enter Marie Curie who through our modern magic, called science, was able to create an invisible weapon in the fight back against that serpent villain: cancer. It is easy to picture her in her laboratory (her MUSEum) and, like Shakespeare, she too invented new words: Radioactivity, Polonium and Radium. She said, *"A scientist in his laboratory is not a mere technician: he is also a child confronting natural phenomena that impress him as though they were fairy tales."* When you are doing what you are born to do, there is an alchemy to it.

I will refer you back to that Goethe quote, "Whatever you can do or dream you can, begin it. Boldness has genius, power, and magic in it," because it is true! You have a scientist here, one of the greatest of all time, telling us that we must work with the imagination of a child and she brings in fairy tales! Again we need that sense of wonder and curiosity to achieve greatness. Curie used her passion and dedication to help the sick. During the First World War, she promoted mobile X-ray machines (they were given the pet name of "Little Curies"). She had a daughter Irene in 1897 and Eve in 1904, but she never stopped working! In her usual stoic nature she reportedly said, "I have frequently been questioned, especially by women, of how I could reconcile family life with a scientific career. Well, it has not been easy."

Moreover, her family could not afford to send her away for education so she took up a governess position in her younger days and sent money for her elder sister to train! Undeterred, she still found time to study and worked her way and that is exactly what she did; on her own terms and on her own merit, she made it to the Sorbonne (Paris) 1891. Oh, and for good measure she had to learn a second language too. By all accounts she did this mostly on an empty stomach, as she had very little money. Legend has it she survived on buttered bread and tea.

In spite of all the obstacles, she graduated and then found love on her very first commission when she met Pierre Curie. They married in 1895. He became her partner in crime and had true alchemy in their work together. They were married for 11 years until he tragically died and Marie found herself a widow with two daughters under ten years old. What a will! What a mind! What a woman! Yes she did go on to win another Nobel Prize and fulfill her destiny, the effects of which are still felt to this day, even while you are reading this!

TALK ABOUT LEGACY!

She is arguably the most famous female scientist of all time. We have ways to treat cancer today because of her; every day her gift to mankind is used to work its magic. After death she is still honoured: in 1995 she and husband Pierre were interred in the Pantheon, I believe she is the only woman to have been given such a national honour. There are nurses working in Marie Curie's name to this day caring for the sick and dying, her charity www.mariecurie.org.uk generates millions each year to provide support for the terminally ill. Her daughter Irene even went on to win the Nobel Prize for chemistry in 1935 too. Marie, it cannot be said that you squandered your 66 years on the planet.

ROCKY FILENAME

MARIE CURIE Marie Curie	
OCCUPATION	Physicist
MADE THEIR ENTRANCE	7th November 1867 Warsaw, Poland
TOOK THEIR LAST BOW	4th July 1934 Passy, France
EDUCATION	Warsaw's "floating university," – was unable to attend the men only university Sorbonne
ORIGINALLY	Maria Sklodowska
AKA	Madame Pierre Curie Madame Maria Curie Madame Curie-Skłodowska
ACHIEVEMENTS (SOME OF..)	First woman to win a Nobel Prize 1903 (Physics). Only person to win the Nobel Prize in two different fields 1911 (Chemistry).

iROCKY

"Everyone believes the world's greatest lie..." says the mysterious old man.
"What is the world's greatest lie?" the little boy asks. The old man replies, "It's this: that at a certain point in our lives, we lose control of what's happening to us, and our lives become controlled by fate. That's the world's greatest lie."
The Alchemist, Paulo Coelho[43]

Here we are, the final chapter, or is it the first chapter? You decide. You are a product of your upbringing, aspirations, educational, friends, family, influencers – what have you become? Are you about to be that base metal that starts to shine and become the gold that you always knew you had in you. This could be a challenge, breaking a habit, doing that thing that you always wanted to do, realising a lifetime dream.

. . . .

---

[43] Paulo Coelho, (2006), *The Alchemist*, Harper Collins

MARATHON DES SABLES (34TH) 2019

Many years ago, as fate would have it, I sat next to MR for the evening dinner awards at the Celtic Manor for an annual conference for financial advisers, circa 2015. He mentioned over dinner that he did this thing called the Marathon Des Sables and had even written a book about it. I was so impressed with his tale, I got on my phone, logged on to Amazon then and there and bought *Running From Shadows*. I can still recall saying to him how awesome it was and that I could never see myself doing anything like that! Running one marathon in the Sahara let alone six was unimaginable – we know now that it all starts with the imagination, seeing it, believing it. However, reading the book didn't do anything to inspire me to do it – it just sounded hard, brutal and as though you would have to be an amazing athlete to survive it. I put it on the shelf and thought, "Good for you Mark, that is some achievement – not for me though." I had no idea that I would be signing up for the 34th Marathon Des Sables, three years later. It was beyond me and something that someone else would do, not me. This is all, of course, pre-IRONMAN® events, pre-finding solace in The MUSEum and pre-realising that we, and only we, put limits on ourselves. However, post-IRONMAN® Wales I decided to go for it and just as when I said YES to IRONMAN® races and some uncanny things started happening, so too with MdS – it was like the Universe was conspiring to make it happen and give some valuable lessons along the way.

First off, Sir Ranulph Fiennes was coming to my town (University of Warwick, to be precise) and giving one of his fantastic talks. Great, I thought, one of the oldest competitors to have completed the MdS he will have some real gems for me. The talk was great, but MdS was only briefly touched upon. I joined the very long book signing queue and waited, waited and waited some more to speak with the great man and get my MdS takeaway. When I finally got to see him, surrounded by his book *Cold*, I asked him for any tips as I was doing the MdS in April. He said, without a hint of comedy, "Buy my book, *Heat*." He could see I was deflated and then came back with, "It is all about the tent mates, if you have a good tent, you will do well." Thank you Sir Ranulph and never a truer word has been spoken.

My next stop was my GP as you have to get a medical form completed by your doctor – a formality, or so I thought! This form has to be completed no more than a month out from the race. I booked an appointment, she booked an ECG etc. But there is no etc, the doctor believed that something was rotten in the state of Denmark or rather the state of my heart and rushed me over to see a cardiologist.

Bear in mind, we were in the lead up to the race and I was flying out in a couple of weeks, yet here we were talking about left ventricular hypertrophy (LVH), the thickening of the wall of my heart, on the left side of my heart! There is something called Athlete's Heart and this can come up from time to time, I was praying that it was this and nothing more. I was prepared for this in some way, as the body takes on oxygen in hard blasts during training and you push yourself, but we weren't talking about that, we were talking about an irregular heartbeat and potentially a life-threatening condition.

I was now having a very clear and present Memento Mori moment, right here, right now – when shown the model of a heart with the potential problem I might have in the cardiologist's office. It was nothing short of having the fear of God put in me and all my heart could do was to be on in it's seemingly previously undetected, unique fashion.

This could be my last Christmas – I went from an ambitious fledgling Ultra runner about to take on arguably one of the world's toughest foot races to "shuffling off" before the winter time – in a heartbeat. Ironically it is a question that I ask my Life Planning clients, "If you went to the doctor and they said you only had 12 months to live, what would you do?" It focuses the mind doesn't it? We all think we have time and when we consider the world without us, or those things that we once thought important, it is amazing what is actually important to you when you see through all the mists of time. What would you be thinking if that was you; what "stuff" do you want to do that you have been putting off? Who would you regret not spending more time with – letting someone know you forgive them, telling someone you love them?

The cardiologist booked me in for an echocardiogram, to hear what was going on and take pictures. At this point, I was still playing it cool and making preparations for the desert – business as usual. I turned up to the appointment and as the friendly nurse started rubbing an ultrasound over my chest, we talked. I explained what I was there for, that this was very unexpected/leftfield, and I did not expect to be there as I was off to Morocco to do the Marathon Des Sables. She said that she had done a bit of running, all the while looking at the screen and taking the photos, measurements etc. Then she started to talk about her bucket list, but looking back from the screen, she said, "But perhaps we shouldn't be talking about that right now." I must confess, my coolness dropped; whatever she saw on the screen from my body meant that bucket lists and endings were not for this time! What had she seen? I asked, as nonchalantly as I could, "Does everything look alright?"

PAUSE............

"Looks okay to me," she said. I didn't ask what that stuff about not discussing bucket lists was all about. I had got my answer, she thought we were looking okay. Now, I had to wait to hear from the cardiologist. She invited me into her office, "Well Mr Bibb," I held my breath, "You have a very good heart." Hallelujah! Whatever came up on the ECG was nothing to worry about and she would happily sign my medical form. Man, that was painful, unexpected and took me to a place I really didn't want to go to. Anyway, mission accomplished, time to get packing!

Not so fast though, my body was making it's protests known; perhaps my 49 years of this, that and the other were taking their toll. I was just going up the stairs as I always do and by the time I got to the top step, I couldn't put weight on my left leg – You what?! I called Craig the local chiropractor and it looked like I had a case of acute sciatica. As we were now in the week just before MdS, I saw him every day. Whilst on the chiropractor's bed he told me about Dr Joe Dispenza and a couple of his books, *You Are The Placebo* and *Being Supernatural*. Craig went on to tell me that Dr Joe was a chiropractor and triathlete, who got hit by a car during a race and broke his back in several places. Based on him being a practicing chiropractor and having a great knowledge of the body, he refused the operation and 'the Harrington Rods' and then self-healed, (yes you read that right!). Check him out. My daughter reminded me of when I smashed my collar bone ('shattered it' was how the doctor phrased it, I was the tender age 22, cycling in London and had my accident right outside The Houses of Parliament) and refused the operation and insisted that I would heal it! And I did! Not in the same league as Dr Joe though, breaking your back, what? Don't forget the magic folks, Dispenza is a man of science but also believes in magic and makes and has made some impossible – possible.

Craig got me match-fit and I bought Dr Joe's books and started learning about his techniques and his world view. I had a clean bill of health all around – two days before jumping on a plane to run 156 miles across the Sahara Desert, self-sufficient with all food and kit with only the daily rations of water supplied by Team MdS.

Jumping on the plane, randomly I sat next to Damien, who was sat next to Johnny. We were all in our own worlds/MUSE, but we got talking – wow! Talk about finding your tribe. Damien had just run another desert Ultra in Oman. He volunteered for a foundation in his spare time and would rescue folk and help out at times of natural disasters or war. Johnny had recently run the North Pole marathon along with several others, and was a professional blogger who had visited every country in the world and was embarking on adventure after adventure after adventure. They both had mates coming along to MdS and would be sharing a tent with them – could I make the grade? I am ever so happy to report that the boys took me in. We gathered with their mates Chris (a former Marine who had recently rowed the Atlantic), Mossy (an Irishman, living in Columbia, who was so pumped up and excited for this race he also made it feel like Christmas Eve). Mossy had originally met Johnny, (an Irishman too) in a gym in Thailand, some years before and their friendship began and Johnny's other friend Anthony (who also was referred to as Geordie), but now like Johnny lives in Thailand. The three of them were great travellers and keen to chalk up as many countries as they could. Just as I was picked up to join the gang, so too was another loner – Paul (also referred to as Scouser), a firefighter. With all of us together, I thought this was something akin to that '80s TV show *Auf Wiedersehen Pet,* but then that would probably make me Barry from the Midlands, perhaps we needed to find our own story, write our own script?

We agreed we'd try and get a tent together and after the long coach ride getting to know each other, we were directed to Tent 52. There was actually a competitor in there already and sleeping. We learnt in the morning his name was Ansar and he was from Dubai. This was when I knew I was going to be okay out there, not only had I fallen in with an amazing bunch of lads, but that name Ansar truly resonated with me, an uncommon name, a name you don't hear too often. When he introduced himself, I had to ask him to repeat it. I had to make sure, you see, Ansar is the name of my oldest friend, when I say oldest I mean from the age of 6! Of all the tents we could have gone to and here I am surrounded by my tribe of adventurers and the talisman of Ansar.

There was so much that happened from that first night to the last day – let me share a couple of my revelations on my R.O.C.K.Y Road along the MdS.

These are the givens: this is our environment for the next nine days, no hiding place, no oasis, sand and 40 degree heat guaranteed, and our lodging is a berber tent (essentially a piece of heavy material that serves as your floor and roof). You get the picture? The next day we completed in-person registration (including that medical form which caused so much heartache, for a heart that was good!). We needed to get our backpacks weighed, with the maximum weight of 15 kilos for all your kit, sleeping bag, food, clothing, the whole shebang.

Recalling what it was like to be in France with a bike and a flat tyre, with nothing but a sewing kit, I was taking no chances in the desert – I packed everything and some. The boys in the tent laughed at all the gear I had – sewing kit, spare head torches – who was this old bloke? (I had at least 10 years on all of them) and was he going to make it? Could he make it with all that stuff? Funny enough, it was my kit that was to come to their rescue on multiple occasions, earning me the title of, "Dad." I had to stitch a backpack, tape up people's feet, exorcise a spider ... (more on that later).

The race each year follows the pattern of day one marathon, day two marathon, day three double marathon, day four rest, day five marathon, day six marathon and then charity run/ walk 5k. At no time did I think I was in trouble, or I might bail here. In fact the opposite, I helped folk and it seemed to make the whole experience easier for me.

So here I am in the desert – even surrounded by great tent mates you cannot help but feel alone, away from your family and those things that form part of your day, your routine. Perhaps that's why you get close to your tent mates and become a band of brothers; enduring together, suffering together, journeying together, albeit each on an individual path through the dunes under the blistering sun. Being ten years older and, to be fair, the slowest of the bunch, I was more like the camel, plodding on working through and they were desert foxes skipping along.

On day three I was getting stronger and moving up from senior camel to "not so senior" camel. I could see a young runner up ahead who was suffering, Davey from the Netherlands, his race number told me. He was hobbling in a bad way (is there ever a good way?), wincing at each step, you get the picture. I stopped, and he told me that his feet needed taping as he was in bad shape and struggling, but none of the aid stations had any tape. I was the right man for this job as I had brought many different tapes just in case but clearly I had brought them for Davey. I had to empty my bag as they were at the bottom and masses of kids flocked from nowhere, with my passport and cash out on display I had to think fast and get that tape otherwise my stay in the desert may be longer than anticipated. The kids were of course just looking for some goodies and my day three sugar rations went to them. We taped Davey up and off he went, with a nod, I yanked the straps tighter and off I set. We will come back to this moment later.

There is another book full of takeaways and unforgettable moments, but what I would like to share over these next paragraphs are three key ones to aid you on your journey: the blind man, the spider, my Grandad.

THE BLIND MAN

I had seen the blind runner with his guide holding hands through the sandy, rocky, dunesy landscape and was bowled over by them – so much so, I tried on the long day to see how long I could run for with my eyes closed! Try it; your other senses get heightened and lasting for more than 30 seconds takes courage – even when you have scouted the land and know that there is nothing for miles and miles ahead. On the last marathon day, we get word this pair are on their way to the finish line. Till the day I die I will never forget them coming over the ridge and with around 500 metres to go the guide must have said something like, "Let's blow the doors off this" and they go from their sedentary walk into a dash for the line, all out. Where my tears came from I don't know as it was hot out there and dehydrating, but looking at these two skipping along the sand, blasting for home, was alchemy, it was magic, it was beautiful. We all clapped and cheered them on. Sometimes it is the blind that can help us see, sometimes it is a guide that leads us to a place that we thought we would never expect to go and sights that we would never see, (DO NOT FORGET THE MAGIC MY PEOPLE). To have missed this moment would have made my time in the desert poorer and it wasn't even my race, it was their race but now it has become part of my library of 'magic moments', under the reference section of "GERONIMO!"

If a blind runner can take on the desert what obstacles/excuses have you come up with to stop you doing that thing that you want to do? There was also a runner with a prosthetic leg, she had to stop every couple of miles to adjust her padding, or to remove sand, and off she goes. We really are our best ally and our worst enemy – not even losing a leg would stop this girl from conquering the Marathon Des Sables. To borrow from Janet Jackson, "What have you excused for me lately?" We have grit, determination and will power but sometimes, that lickle shin becuase you got shinsplintz 10 years ago, that hip, that knee, that shoulder, we must endure – life is not easy and suffering is part of it, don't limit yourself! We have held up many, some old, some new to demonstrate that whatever you want is within you. Don't listen to the doubters, the naysayers, listen to that voice in you that says I CAN.

THE SPIDER

I will come to the spider in a moment, but did you know it took Ed Sheeran ten years to become a billionaire? Whether you did his music or not, listen to his story; his alchemic moment came while watching Eric Clapton perform Layla at a concert for the Queen. He told himself he wanted to play like that and he worked on the guitar until he became a megastar. I ask you what could you do in the next 10 years to reveal your greatness? He could have made excuses, I'll never be that good... It will take years and years... OR he could pick it up and get to work.

Ed is not unique, he is a great talent, but we all have this inside we just need to find it and let it out. There are many Ed's working in a factory because they let the excuses be their story. It's akin to being scared of spiders; they are tiny and in the UK, where I am sitting writing this for you, no spider will harm you, yet we let them get into our minds and because of our imagination and scale of our minds, once a spider phobia gets in there, they become monsters. THEY CANNOT HURT YOU, you know this, but the way they move brrrrrrrrrrrrrrr, this unsettles you, you are a giant, a titan in comparison and could squish it in a heartbeat and yet it is you who shudders, asks for help and tells that person that you are scared of spiders, reinforcing this really odd situation. Imagine that you are outside of yourself filming this moment – it is laughable isn't it? What are you scared of? You will come up with lots of "excuses," it's hairy, the way it eats, it makes webs, but none actually give validation to this irrational fear.

Returning to the Sahara, on the last night there was a small awards ceremony, brought to a swift end due to a sandstorm that was whipping up. My Tent Team and I headed back to the berber tent, talking about the day and getting ready for lights out. We all snuggled into the sleeping bags when Paul's head torch caught something on the tent roof, perhaps four feet above his face. I'm not sure who started the screaming but Tent 52 didn't just have a spider, we had something that could have easily sat in one of the Alien films. It was big, white and plastic looking but this was not a toy spider, a violin spider or sac spider perhaps. Certainly one you don't want to dance with.

We had no time to ask questions. As the Tent called me Dad, naturally I had to rid the tent of this demon, aided by Chris, who wanted to "flick it out." I asked for calm and whilst the spider crawled along the tent roof, now towards me, I grabbed one of the large discarded empty water bottles and rapidly began cutting the bottom off it – no one was going to be "flicking" this thing, I wanted to make sure he was captured and then taken as far away from camp as possible!

Our noise had stirred a lot of the camp. I now held up the bottle to catch the interloper and Marine Chris shepherded it towards our makeshift trap. Success! We caught it, but it was a big one and had to use a flat rock to get it in and keep it inside the bottle – looking at it through the plastic was not reassuring, this was a bad boy. One of the MdS security guards came over to see what all the hullabaloo was about and when I showed him the prisoner, he immediately backed away and all he said was "Fire, Fire." I was not going to end the toughest and yet most exhilarating race of my life by frying this creature, that was not how I wanted this frisson in the desert to end. The point here, dear reader, is we all let the "spider" in and give it the power. Fortunately I had been baptised "Dad" by the boys and so my instincts were to look after them. The lesson here from the

Sahara is don't fear the spider, don't let it in your head, use something equally as strong, to not only survive it but thrive through it. Look out for those mind spiders that can paralyse you with fear. Don't forget you have a role to play – do not let the spider win, bottle it up and deal with it.

MY GRANDAD

It was during the dawn on the double marathon day that it happened. You could hear the camels waking and with the sun I seemed to get renewed vigour, through the night we had been following glow sticks and hoped that they did indeed light the way – now I know it was Patrick Bauer (Marathon Des Sables creator), waiting for me by a small stream. There were some stepping stones, his jeep parked up, and there he was arm extended to guide me across the stepping stones. It was probably fatigue, but I saw my Grandad, arm out giving me aid and helping me to the end of my longest day, even after I heard myself say, "Merci" and run on, I ask myself, if that was my Grandad (who I lost on December 22nd 1986). I was buoyed and picked up my pace, running past some fellow athletes, one who was antipodean shouted to my back, "* * * * man, go for it" and so I did.

This was my biggest fear coming out here: would I have the minerals to not only do each run by myself and see what demons come during the solitude, but to do the double marathon. Going ultra alone would always be the big test and I had endured, I kept running, made the checkpoint and found my way to home, Tent 52. All the camp were in and asleep, but as soon as I turned up, they all shot up out of their beds. There were hugs and "Rocky!" and "Dad you made it!" I did detect relief from the boys who were only lightly sleeping, worrying about the old man of the camp.

Now, at the MdS they have a tent devoted to feet – 'Doc Trotters' – where nightly runners are patched up. I'm happy to report that I didn't have one blister, not one. Was this because I was on my quest, following my bliss? Or did I just invest in the right socks? Questions... We will never know!

Something equally as profound happened on the very last day. This is when we do a charity run, some six miles, and Tent 52 decided we would walk as one of our number couldn't run anymore and also I think it was because a part of us didn't want it to end. We got very close, very quickly and we were all stripped down to our bare bones; the desert doesn't care what car you drive, how big your house is, if you've got daddy issues, how much money in the bank – none of that. You had what you were wearing, your backpack and your character, that is all you take into the desert and that is what you leave it with (as well as hopefully, some lessons and that character chipped away to define 'YOU', that wee bit more).

I mentioned that I packed for every eventuality and as we crossed the line together we hugged, and then as we walked to the transport a little child came up to me and asked for something. My food was depleted, I had shared what I had with this little man's brethren on the route. He (cheekily) pointed to my sunglasses and I smiled and handed them over. My Little cousin had travelled all the way to surprise me on the finish line and I started telling him about a book I read to my kids at Christmas, 'The Fourth King'. It's the tale of the fourth Magi but he doesn't make it to the stable in time, as he keeps helping those he encounters on his journey. It is a lovely read. As I was recounting some of the examples of my "encounterings," who was waiting for me? None other than Davey from the Netherlands, the chap who I helped tape up when he was struggling. Bear in mind that Tent 52 had had a leisurely walk that morning to finish our Marathon Des Sables and this chap had been waiting for me for some time. Seeking me out, he shook my hand, gave me a hug and thanked me for stopping and helping him that day as he was ready to quit. Then he headed to get on the coach for the six-hour journey back to civilization. I looked at my cuz, with this testimonial underlining what I do; I help people – I can't help it. That night back at the hotel we learned that I had the heaviest backpack and was given an MDS award! A 49 year old, who only did his first ultra run that same year, made it through the desert and managed to help a few souls on the way – not a bad way to lead one's life.

....

BLOG FOR THE KINDER INSTITUTE 2019 – MY MARATHON DES SABLES

There is nothing special about me and just as Charles Dickens was adamant that we understood that, "Marley was dead to begin with" at the start of *A Christmas Carol*, you have to believe this or there will be no magic. There is nothing special about me. I am 5'7, some 13 stone (85kgs), and in my 48 years on the planet I have no sporting badges or trophies of merit from my younger days. Have you got that picture in your head now? I am Joe Ordinary. So let us begin and hopefully some sparks may fly, some "stuff" occur and you may find yourself being an Ordinary too, but doing something "extra" Ordinary. But YOUR kind of extra.

The Marathon Des Sables (MdS) has been called the "world's toughest foot race"– whether it is or not, is not an issue we need to debate here, but six marathons in seven days, being self-sufficient (i.e carrying all your kit and food for the seven days through the Sahara), for most, would put the fear of God in them – so why am I standing on the start line of this, the 34th MdS? There are several people I could hold to account for this, Joseph Campbell who wrote that we should "Follow our Bliss," George Kinder when he reminds us to live "on purpose" and to dig for the treasures that we all have buried inside of us or a much overlooked screenwriter who in 1976 wrote a film that was to become a friend of mine, the writer also said, "I may not be the tallest, fastest or prettiest but I just want to take a shot at it and then I'll know." The film was called Rocky, eponymously written and played by Sylvester Stallone.

Everyone loves the story of the underdog, everyone loves the Hero's Journey (as Campbell has framed it). You know the tale as it is the premise for most movies that you've ever seen; someone living a life but knowing that inside them there is more. Picture Luke Skywalker in *Star Wars Episode IV*, Neo in *The Matrix* and even good old George Bailey from *It's a Wonderful Life*. So too did I feel, come on, as we all do, that there is just something, some act that has not been done, a box that is unchecked, unfinished business, 'stuff in the basement', that you have to get done, to live with intention and get closer to what fulfilled might look like for you. I arrived in the desert armed only with my alter ego 'Rocky' and a whole backpack full of expedition foods and my vision to do the Marathon Des Sables, not for me, but for my four kids, to show them that anything is possible; for my clients, for them to believe that it is doable to run your own business, help as many people as you can on the way and do something like a multi-stage ultra marathon; and for my friends, to borrow from Coldplay, we really are "diamonds taking shape" – we all have greatness inside us.

But hold on, I hear you say as the obstacles start talking to you, "you must be able to train a lot and I don't have time for that" (I didn't train a lot for this, because I couldn't, lots of reasons, but for now let me just say even in the week before the MdS I had to see a chiropractor everyday). "I am too old" (the oldest competitor was 83, with many 60 and 70 year olds taking part). "My knees", or the like – let me tell you, I saw two athletes with prosthetic limbs not only start MdS, but rip it up, and there was a blind chap too.

So, we have the vision. You have already come up with why you couldn't possibly ever do anything like run 150 miles through the desert and those have been silenced by those that have come before you and took that road, or rather that sand dune, less travelled. Please understand I am not recruiting for the Marathon Des Sables, this is just another story of how something which looks like an Odyssey, something that is impossible has been made possible and has been done by some 30,000 people who got through, over, under or around their obstacles. So if you have something you want to do in your life, do it, don't wait.

What is your Marathon of the sand? What is that thing that you have buried in the sands of time, as "life" has just got in the way? Just as the sands of our hourglass keep falling through, will you look at the time past as a big insurmountable desert, impossible to cross with all your baggage (you know what I am talking about)? Or use those sands of time to count, to mean something, to be a sand dune that you can strive up valiantly and make your time count or use the voice in this piece to help you dig and find your buried treasure in the sand? You already know where your X marks the spot, go to that island where you cleverly buried it and have since, cleverly, come up with lots of reasons not to visit that secret island again and indeed, even hidden the map. Please get out your treasure maps and go to get your treasure, whatever it is, wherever it is. The journey may be arduous and you can talk yourself out of it easily, so this is your call to action: suit up and go do that thing you just have got to do, it's ready and waiting for you. "Maktub," as some say crossing the finishing line here in Morocco, "It is written".

EXERCISE TIME:
WHO ARE YOUR FIVE?

Now if it's true, that we are the sum total of the five people we spend the most time with then I encourage you to just take five! Take five of our case studies and let them, their life, their journey, their struggles inform your life. My Tent 52 mates helped me through the MdS but that was easy as a tribe, as we were on the same journey, with the same start and same finish line. We are more often on our own with the starting and finishing lines of our own design.

We don't have a tent full of our tribe members, BUT what you can take, what you can always take, is the tribal wisdom and that is what I hope and pray that you can lean into from investing your time with us.

THE R.O.C.K.Y ROAD
FOR MARIE CURIE

Rise – Another force of nature that neither geography, language, being unable to get a university education nor being a woman in a very much man's world – double Nobel Prize winner and much more; widow, single mother Marie Curie.

Obstacle – With no money and with there being no place for a woman like her, she was denied a higher education.

Choices – She finds a way through, she finds a place to study, an Underground University; a reminder to us that sometimes, we have to go lower before we rise.

Kaizen – She works her way to the Sorbonne and gets a double degree and this paves the way for the two Nobel Prizes. The habit of hard work gets her through bringing up two daughters after the death of her husband. Her dedication and drive from a young start became a lasting life skill.

You – So what can Curie teach you? When the world says, "This is men only" as they did to her, do you fold? Do you give up on your dreams when someone says no? Look back at how her actions affect us to this day – what will your actions be doing around the world, 70, 100, 200 years after you have gone? The Alchemy truly happened when she met Pierre and their work went on to create something epochal. Who do you have in your life that, when you are together the sparks fly and the magic happens? If you don't have your own Pierre, then perhaps you should find one. Can I ask you, when you hear about the struggles of someone who works and scrapes their way to another country, to learn in another language, who becomes a mother, yet still excels as a woman in a male-dominated world with no money, no sponsor and obstacles at every turn, how does this make you feel about your "perceived" challenges. She became a widow with two young girls and did it all anyway, so what is stopping you?

. . . .

MUSEUM OF MOMENTUM TOUR

This is our last journey to The MUSEum together. Just as Curie headed to the lab to work her magic, we head to our Muse to battle our confusions and get clarity. Our mental boardroom is complete, we have had athletes, artists and now our scientist. They all came from different times and backgrounds, all had their challenges, but they are all defined by what they did and not by what stopped them, how they overcame, endured. With Curie it was all about process, if you listen ever so carefully you can hear her. Whispers from Marie Curie: "*I believe that Science has great beauty. A scientist in his laboratory is not a mere technician; he is also a child confronting natural phenomena that impress him as though they were fairy tales.*"

But Marie, we are all busy people, how can we take a short-cut? She answers, "*I was taught that the way of progress was neither swift nor easy.*"

There you have your answer, you need to work on you. Just like going to the gym a couple of times a year will not make you fit, reading a book alone will not make you wise – it is what you do with the wisdom of the book that will create good habits, (replacing some of the unwanted ones!). Curie made it happen for herself, time and time again her efforts carried through to the next generation with her daughter winning a Nobel Prize too!

It is interesting to note that apart from her science legacy, we also have the Marie Curie nurses carrying her name and the drive for making the world better, however the skies are looking. The daffodil is the symbol for Marie Curie nurses, and her work continues on, and on. "They're a symbol of spring, new beginnings and rebirth." Meredith Niles, Executive Director of Fundraising and Engagement at Marie Curie.

Just take a step back now and survey how far we have come. You have a map and some key compass points are the Hero's Journey – this is everyone's journey. Our 12 Hall of Famers had to take risks and leave "The Ordinary World." They all found and worked with someone who helped bring them and/or their talents on, and the rest they say is history, BUT before we ourselves are confined to history, Let's Rock! Let's rock our comfort zone, let us take those brave steps down our own R.O.C.K.Y Road to success.

Most people talk about Michelangelo's Sistine Chapel as the big show but it is the wall at the back of the room in that chapel that is his more profound work: 'The Day of Judgement'. The journey to this point is your Day of Judgement – make a choice, decide, you will surprise yourself with what you are capable of, I promise you. I hope those iRocky's have got you thinking, "He sounds like a normal bloke and he did a few things, I will give .... a go." Do it and see where, when you start down that road, it will take you. Do not leave another "Road not taken." You have test cases here and my testimonials, so now go and test yourself.

I leave you with hope of new beginnings. You really do have it in you, my Grandparents knew it all along, they kept telling me over and over: "You can do anything you put your mind to."

AFTERWORD

So you have made it thus far, how far do you want to go? If you hadn't heard it before, if that giant in you is still sleeping, THIS is it, this is your call to action. The adventures, suffering and obstacles that you have read now and gone through with me are to get you on the path for your adventures, your Hero's Journey – we all have it in us. It is not reserved for a select few – it's in me, in you, in us all. What are you going to do? Now is the time! Find and release your alter ego, dream big and start on the path. Take a coach/mentor and do the audacious thing you were born to do. That is why you are here!

I wish you a full life of adventure, finding yourself or that truer self like Goggins, challenging what's possible like Team Hoyt, standing the test of time like Shakespeare, with people still revelling in your work like Michelangelo... You have read this stuff now, so what are you waiting for? A Renaissance. What does it mean to you? Rebirth? Or just some old word that happened a long time ago? My friends, we can all have a rebirth, at any time, at any age – look at what Weight Watchers does for a lot of people; they lose a stone and feel 10 years younger, they enjoy clothes shopping and not getting a fright when they see themselves in a mirror. Someone gets made redundant and is forced to reassess where they are and perhaps make a new career choice, or even start their own business. What about those of us who have lost a loved one through death or divorce?

You do find something in you that helps/makes you carry on and it is to this part of you that this book speaks.

Nascent is that rich word and it means your unrealised potential – yes it is unrealised, you haven't found it yet, but no matter who you are or where you are, it is within you. Sometimes it requires an epochal moment for it to come out. Sometimes you just need to read a book about transformation or discovery and shazam, that part of you has awoken and your journey has begun.

That was my *why* for picking up the pen initially, but it has morphed greatly from that original purpose because this isn't about me anymore. That was only the genesis, the "I" of the biographer has moved to "You" the audience, the future actions are all on you now. The gauntlet has been thrown, let's see what you can do. My *why* is for you to live the best life you can. The R.O.C.K.Y Project is here to remove obstacles and enable you to make the choice. I sincerely hope you get your money's worth reader, as you move from passive to participant in the Olympics of your life. Have that experience that *you* want, whether it is white water rafting, your first 5K run, taking up painting, learning to swim, cycling from Lands' End to John O'Groats or seeing the orangutans in Borneo. Remember what Mickey said to Rocky (Rocky II): "What's can't? There ain't no can'ts, there's no can'ts."

Apologies for the repetition, it's my ploy to get the message through. Did it work? What about another mentor to help you answer the call to action: "Do or do not, there is no try," (Yoda from Star Wars Episode V: The Empire Strikes Back). So you have the picture now, you know that you are in the picture and you have had two of the best celluloid mentors to tell it like it is.

Hopefully your life is rich in whatever sense "rich" means to you. You also know that once you have "that thing," something else puts itself on to your to-do list. The legacy of this book will not be how many copies it has sold, it will be the effect it has, starting with YOU. Not just Random acts of Kindness (RAOK), but with us all getting a greater sense of being significant and inspiring others, as Zig Ziglar said, "You will get all you want in life, if you help enough other people get what they want."[44]

So we started Chapter One with "Journey." Is this the end or the start of one for you? Can you hear that call to action get louder? Like a drum, its beat quickens, its bass getting louder – can you ignore it? Do not leave it too late, time passes, there are some exercises for you here and some poetry, some universal truths, but just like going to gym a couple of times a year, reading a couple of books a year is just dusting off the cobwebs; you need to work on you, you need to make that work Kaizen, it never ends. As with this book, right now, it is all in your hands.

Here are my details if you feel that I am someone you could work with **therockyprojectexperience@gmail.com** or even if you want to give me your feedback, so I can write an

[44] Zig Ziglar, (2000), See You At The Top, Pelican, 25th anniversary edition, first published 1974

even better book, with an even bigger impact, next time. Seize the day my brothers and sisters, before the day seizes you!

These pages are not here by accident and neither are you! The following are for your notes – some of the words and thoughts that resound within you, here you can let it all out! Please don't leave these empty, your story has not yet finished, fill the pages and "Do not go gentle into that good night!"

EPILOGUE

Remember I told you I was "retired" at IRONMAN® Bolton back in 2019 – well rather than that being my swan song, in 2021 I decided to take on three IRONMAN® full-distance races in three months, one of which was The 255.

. . . .

Race Report on The 255
(World's longest single-day triathlon,
255 kilometres in 18 hours) 8.8.2021:

Cov Tri, g'day one and all, thought I would share my experience from last Sunday. Again for full disclosure I am a back of the pack athlete who only took up triathlon five years ago. I signed up for this one, truth be told, as I misread the details – 140.6 miles to 158 miles – around a 12 per cent hike, bring it. That was my first mistake; the variations from the IRONMAN® triathlon's full distance are an extra 0.7 mile of swimming, 12 miles on the bike and five miles of running – that didn't sound too much extra to me, in my simple world, but when you add "the weather" to that equation, the game changes. Held at the

Goodwood Motor Racing Circuit, Chichester (and a 1.5km bike to the start line not included in the distances) – it looked like it would be a beautiful English summer's day but no, early on in the swim the wind turned up and I almost said to myself, "I don't think we are in Kansas anymore, Toto." Cov Tri taught me to front crawl back in 2016 and I thought I was doing a good job and sighting was good, but the wind was so strong it was flapping the large buoys about so swimming close to them meant getting bopped on the head – this was a lake swim but I still managed to get sea sick on lap three of four.

I persevered and managed to get out in 2:27 (yes, you read that right), second to last man out of the lake, chuffed though that that was my longest swim. I suit up for the bike – 52 laps of Goodwood for my longest ever cycle. What became quickly demoralising was that EVERYONE was overtaking me – there were relay teams doing the same distance as well as us hardy solo entrants. Even when I noticed I was doing around 20 miles an hour on the "mostly" flat course, others were whizzing by, lap after lap, after lap. I did manage to make up a little time, but I was the last man out on the track. The mini crowd that was there got right behind me though (sympathy vote I am sure) and kept cheering for my nine solo laps. I eventually got out onto the track for the 31 mile run, just 10 laps of the circuit. Well, this is a long enough report as is, so heading straight to the "numbers": 100 souls signed up for this race, only 75 got to the start line and only 51 finished. I was the 51st man – and considering my sporting background and being 51 years old, I will take it! Cov Tri should definitely put in at least a relay team for this next year as those guys were having fun and it was great to see them all run across the line together. It was a long day for me, finishing in 17 hours 40 mins. My goal was just to finish the race, so coming last was okay for me — mission accomplished. On to IRONMAN® Hamburg in T-Minus 16 days! Seizing the day my Triathlete Brethren! As I hope you are too!! Dare greatly!!!

Rocky.

BIBLIOGRAPHY

BOOKS

Can't Hurt Me by David Goggins

A Life Without Limits by Chrissie Wellington

You Can't Take It With You by Jane & Mike Tomlinson

The Alchemist by Paulo Coelho

The Hero's Journey: Joseph Campbell on His Life and Work by Phil Cousineau & Stuart Brown

The Hero with a Thousand Faces by Joseph Campbell

The Brave Athlete by Simon Marshall & Lesley Paterson

The Chimp Paradox by Dr Steve Peters

Ego Is The Enemy by Ryan Holiday

Grit by Angela Duckworth

Start With Why by Simon Sinek

BIBLIOGRAPHY

Delivering Happiness by Tony Hsieh

The Icarus Deception by Seth Godin

A Whole New Mind by Daniel H Pink

You are the Placebo by Dr Joe Dispenza

Becoming Supernatural by Dr Joe Dispenza

The Rise of Superman by Steven Kotler

Rich Dad Poor Dad by Robert T.Kiyosaki

Illusions by Richard Bach

Jonathan Livingston Seagull by Richard Bach

12 Rules for Life by Jordan Peterson

7 Habits of Highly Effective People by Stephen Covey

The Fourth King by Ted Sieger

King of The World by David Reminick

Legacy by James Kerr

The Hobbit by JRR Tolkien

Running from Shadows by Mark Roe

The Death of Ivan Ilych by Leo Tolstoy

FILMS

The Matrix

Star Wars

It's a Wonderful Life

Scrooge

Marvel Cinematic Universe (MCU)

Dead Poets Society

POEMS

Do not go gentle into that good night by Dylan Thomas

The Road not taken by Robert Frost

If by Rudyard Kipling

Tichborne's Elegy by Chidiock Tichborne

ABOUT THE AUTHOR

Michael Bibb is a husband (20+ years), father, trusted adviser, coach, IRONMAN® athlete and Ultrarunner. In his spare time he likes to think about that future time of keeping bees and growing his own veg, but as long as business owners and entrepreneurs want to keep working with him and help them live more of the life they want to, the bees and the veggies will just have to wait – he enjoys the client work too much.

He is the Founder of The R.O.C.K.Y Project. Please get in touch if any of this book has resonated with you and had a positive impact on your life, email **therockyprojectexperience@gmail.com** or visit our website **www.therockyproject.co.uk**

After growing up in Coventry and seeing a bit of the world as a young actor, he then studied at The Guildhall School of Music and Drama, Barbican (London) gaining BA (Hons) and The Chairman's Prize. He has run a bar, was asked to be a coach, became a professional actor, was asked to be a coach again, became a regulated Pension Transfer Specialist and again asked to be a coach – you see the theme here...

His Desert Island Discs are currently:

U2 One, SIA Chandelier, BILL CONTI Gonna fly now, VAN MORRISON Brown Eyed Girl, PRINCE Purple Rain, EMINEM 'Till I collapse, QUEENS OF THE STONE AGE No one knows, FLEETWOOD MAC Go your own way.

Whilst not a magician, he does look out for magic and relishes those "Shazam!" moments, some of which have been documented in this book.

Printed in Great Britain
by Amazon